Getting Results with Curriculum Mapping

edited by Heidi Hayes Jacobs

Association for Supervision and Curriculum Development
Alexandria, Virginia USA

Association for Supervision and Curriculum Development
1703 N. Beauregard St. • Alexandria, VA 22311-1714 USA
Phone: 800-933-2723 or 703-578-9600 • Fax: 703-575-5400
Web site: http://www.ascd.org E-mail: member@ascd.org

Gene R. Carter, *Executive Director;* Nancy Modrak, *Director of Publishing;* Julie Houtz, *Director of Book Editing & Production;* Ernesto Yermoli, *Project Manager;* Shelley Kirby, *Senior Graphic Designer;* Valerie Sprague & Keith Demmons, *Desktop Publishing Specialists;* Tracey A. Franklin, *Production Manager*

All Web links in this book are correct as of the publication date below but may have become inactive or otherwise modified since that time. If you notice a deactivated or changed link, please e-mail books@ascd.org with the words "Link Update" in the subject line. In your message, please specify the Web link, the book title, and the page number on which the link appears.

ASCD Member Book, No. FY05-2 (November 2004, PC). ASCD Member Books mail to Premium (P), Comprehensive (C), and Regular (R) members on this schedule: Jan., PC; Feb., P; Apr., PCR; May, P; July, PC; Aug., P; Sept., PCR; Nov., PC; Dec., P.

Paperback ISBN: 0-87120-999-3 • ASCD product # 104011 • List Price: $25.95 ($19.95 ASCD member price, direct from ASCD only) e-books ($25.95): netLibrary ISBN 1-4166-0156-2 • ebrary ISBN 1-4166-0157-0

Library of Congress Cataloging-in-Publication Data
Getting results with curriculum mapping / edited by Heidi Hayes Jacobs.
    p. cm.
  Includes bibliographical references and index.
  ISBN 0-87120-999-3 (alk. paper)
  1. Teacher participation in curriculum planning—United States. I. Jacobs, Heidi Hayes.
II. Association for Supervision and Curriculum Development.

LB2806.15.G48 2004
375'.001—dc22

2004016184

10 09 08 07 06 05 04   12 11 10 9 8 7 6 5 4 3 2 1

Getting Results with Curriculum Mapping

Foreword

Curriculum mapping addresses some of the most critical questions for any work team:

- Who is doing what?
- How does our work align with our goals?
- Are we operating efficiently and effectively?

Educators who nurture the growth of each child form a work team from prekindergarten to postsecondary school. They take their work seriously and are aware of the awesome responsibility of preparing children for life roles. Yet, as an institution, education is a business in which teachers at one level have little knowledge of the curriculum and instruction that takes place at other levels. Teachers follow the district or school curriculum and use required materials, but they have little opportunity to share a dialogue with fellow teachers about what they are teaching and how the overall educational program is working for students.

Besides the problem of time for professional dialogue, the work team must deal with problems in the curriculum. Teachers purchase supplementary materials over time to bolster this or that topic or skill, or they move to a different grade level and take favorite materials with them. Eventually, the curriculum becomes cluttered with "stuff" that may or may not support educational efficiency or effectiveness.

Curriculum mapping is an invaluable tool that can help schools clean their closets. Since Dr. Heidi Hayes Jacobs wrote her best-selling book, *Mapping the Big Picture: Integrating Curriculum and Assessment K–12* (1997a), schools have been sifting, sorting, aligning, and organizing their curricular closets. Teachers create individual curriculum maps that identify by calendar months the topics, skills, and assessments they are addressing. They then analyze individual maps through the grades and courses to assess vertical articulation and alignment to academic standards.

Primarily, mapping enables teachers to identify gaps, redundancies, and misalignments in the curriculum and instructional program and to foster dialogue among teachers about their work. As Dr. Jacobs points out in Chapter 1 of this book, however, curriculum mapping is ultimately targeted to the outcomes of "measureable improvement in student performance . . . and . . . a process for ongoing curriculum and assessment review."

This book, *Getting Results with Curriculum Mapping*, paves the way for educators involved with, or considering, curriculum mapping projects. In Chapter 1, editor and contributor Dr. Jacobs sets the stage for the field reports that address frequently asked questions, shares stories about implementation and strategies from individual schools and school districts, and then paints the power of and shows the need for curriculum mapping.

A key feature of this exciting new book is that it represents diverse voices from around the country. We read stories about curriculum mapping initiatives from public, private, and special education populations; from principals and central office leaders who are charged with planning, implementing, and motivating staff members; and from the teachers who share, evaluate, align, and refine their curricular and instructional programs.

In Chapter 8, for example, Joseph Lachowicz, who works in an alternative education program in Pittsburgh, Pennsylvania, describes how curriculum mapping has critically supported the work in 11 distinct alternative education populations drawn from both court-based and community-based programs. Because most teachers in those programs teach multiple subjects, mapping has allowed them to align the critical standards, skills, activities, and assessments; to integrate across subjects when feasible; and to communicate with other teachers and their administrator on a month-to-month basis.

The contributors to this book honestly report the low points and high points in the mapping process: low points when some teachers resist, when the direction becomes confused, or when lack of time makes the job appear overwhelming; and high points when teachers become excited about their jobs as they collaborate about their work and discover where they can make connections with fellow teachers.

Through the stories in this book, strong themes of leadership and process emerge that can change the efforts of any organization.

Leadership

Leadership is the key to successful change. As Dr. Valerie Truesdale states in Chapter 2, "Initiatives are not successful because they are not sustained." Leadership is critical to sustaining the efforts of the work teams. Leaders set expectations; see that goals, tasks, and deadlines are set and met; encourage talk about initiatives to keep them alive; and value the work efforts by finding time for teachers to meet and accomplish required tasks.

In Chapter 6, Mary Ann Holt draws on her experiences with curriculum mapping in her roles as principal and curriculum consultant to provide administrators with practical advice on (1) creating a planning team within the staff to support initiatives, (2) providing training to other staff members, and (3) presenting a clear definition of mapping to the staff. (You will enjoy Holt's "treasure hunt" activity to help staff members understand the point of mapping.) Holt shares strategies for answering questions from the staff, for determining how to free up teacher time for mapping, and for using checklists to keep teachers focused during the initial phases of mapping.

Process

Leaders pay attention to *process* when introducing and implementing an initiative. Curriculum mapping as a process relies on the ability of the work team to collaborate, conceptualize, compromise, and listen. Throughout the chapters of this book, readers will find quality examples of process planning—from goal setting, to task and time line development, to mapping review strategies, and to motivating and facilitating work teams.

Getting Results with Curriculum Mapping is both a timely and timeless resource for all educators who need to revisit process. It reminds us to periodically sift, sort, and organize, and it saves us from spinning our wheels by showing us the way. The contributions from the various roles, schools, and perspectives encourage us to work smarter by using technology as a mapping tool. Dr. Jacobs presents a new and exciting view for the use of technology in curriculum and instruction. She provides practical suggestions for using technology to map, evaluate, share, refine, and alter curricula that can replace or reduce the time-consuming, paper-eating sea of handwritten wall charts.

In Chapter 5, Stephen O'Neil, who was the curriculum director at Minnehaha Academy, a private school in Minneapolis, Minnesota, describes how effective computers can be in curriculum mapping. He shares one of his faculty member's reflections and advice:

"getting [the] curriculum together in a computer format [allows it to] be easily updated in the future. [Mapping] is a 'fluid' process."

In Chapter 7, Bena Kallick and James Wilson contrast the effectiveness and efficiency of "computer software mapping" with unwieldy "paper mapping." They remind us that communication is enhanced and curriculum can be more effectively coordinated when teachers can see the content and skills being taught by others in their grade level or department. Computer technology allows teachers and administrators to quickly and easily see not only the particular content and skills being taught, but also the frequency with which the content and skills appear across grade levels.

Kallick and Wilson make another strong point by suggesting that computer technology can be used at the district level to bring coherence to the overall educational program in today's standards-based environment. Site-based management practices led to disparate types and interpretations of data. Conversely, computer technology that shows systemic views of curriculum maps can ensure overall program coherence and can lead to stronger educational programming for all students.

This helpful new book reflects a deepening of the mapping process by looking at applications and experiences from the field, and it answers the myriad questions that inevitably arise with any new initiative. Emphasizing the bedrock premise that mapping "just makes sense," the chapters deal with practical issues such as getting started, consensus building, and rethinking the way schools are organized to make decisions.

This book supports grassroots curriculum evaluation and decision making. Building administrators and teachers—the work teams closest to the students—evaluate and determine the best curriculum plans for students. In the process, such work teams become intimately familiar with what students need to know, understand, and be able to do.

In Chapter 4, Jennie Johnson and Dr. Ann Johnson share the mapping journey of the school district in Ankeny, Iowa, a strong district that became even stronger. They describe the critical role of building curriculum facilitators: two at each elementary school and three at each secondary school. These facilitators performed many tasks, including setting goals with their staff members and principals and determining inservice needs, products to be developed, and time lines to be met. They ensure that the initiative for mapping and program improvement doesn't fizzle out by monitoring the mapping work and providing the critical quality control component. Curriculum frameworks for the Ankeny Community School District, based on the data from each school's map, were aligned with standards and assessments, bringing coherence across district programs.

The Ankeny District provided the time and training needed to get the job done well. It also altered the focus of ongoing Saturday classes for staff development or graduate credit to include training in curriculum mapping and other related district initiatives. As Johnson and Johnson state, "Curriculum mapping became the hub that focused the work of the district on enhancing student achievement. Every aspect of the work in the district emanated from that hub, and the hub served as an organizing force for bringing together the group of dedicated professionals . . . allow[ing] teachers and administrators to become dreamers and confident risk-takers in their quest to help all students become independent and lifelong learners."

A strong curriculum is the foundation for strong teaching and learning. Curriculum mapping *is* the logical hub for the work of school improvement. When teachers realize the benefits of curriculum mapping, they say, "Why didn't we do this years ago? I finally know what students are learning before and after their year with me, and I now have a curriculum that is clear, uncluttered, and focused."

—H. Lynn Erickson
Curriculum Consultant and Author

Acknowledgments

Colleagues create new pathways in a shared profession. It is as if we walk along a common trail of practice and consider the possible directions we might go. Each and every author in this book has been a resourceful and energetic colleague. The people at ASCD have been tremendously supportive of this work, and I value their ability to take the long view for our learners. It has been a joy to work with the insightful and experienced Joyce McLeod as our ASCD development editor. I wish to acknowledge the influence of one of my mentors, Dr. Abraham Tannenbaum from Teachers College, Columbia University, who has shown intellectual persistence over a remarkable lifetime career. My assistant, Kathy Scoli, personifies reliability and competence, making each workday a pleasure.

As a genuine 21st-century shift in our practice, mapping requires knowledge and courage. I am indebted to the countless teachers, administrators, technology programmers, and staff developers in the field who have shared their suggestions as we journey through curriculum mapping. In particular, I want to thank my family, Jeffrey, Rebecca, and Matt, for their constant love and support. They are always with me.

—Heidi Hayes Jacobs

1 Development of a Prologue

Setting the Stage for Curriculum Mapping

Heidi Hayes Jacobs

"Prologue" in Greek means "before the action of the play." Setting the stage, literally and figuratively, elevates the attention of all participants—the actors, the director, and the intended audience. As I have observed schools and districts develop their mapping projects, ample preparation time has characterized the most effective attempts. Clearly, the most successful education settings have crafted a prologue to their actions. They used advance scouting reports, research, and discussion groups before they applied substantial effort and energy. Then they identified key people and charged those people with advance planning for a new and dynamic shift in curriculum decision making.

Those effective districts and schools gave themselves permission to find out what they needed to know in order to create the conditions for success. Rather than acting on a strange statement that runs through some education circles—"We have the right to fail"—these people said, "We have the right to succeed." Rather than starting a mapping initiative by abruptly declaring that "We are going to start curriculum mapping, folks," the leadership teams and district personnel began by looking at the needs of their specific student population. They began by finding out how other schools used curriculum mapping to help with teaching and learning. Mapping can be an extraordinary vehicle to meet carefully defined needs. Curriculum mapping is a procedure for collecting data about the operational curriculum in a school or district referenced directly to the calendar. Mapping provides the basis for authentic examination of that database in conjunction with assessment information about learners. Curriculum mapping is best carried out electronically so that both communication and revisions can be immediate.

Defining Success with Mapping

Success in a mapping program is defined by two specific outcomes: measurable improvement in student performance in the targeted areas, and the institutionalization of mapping as a process for ongoing curriculum and assessment review.

Improvement in student performance can be in developing academic skills, but it can also focus on developing character traits, aesthetic awareness, or athletic prowess. Students in any given environment need a range of proficiencies to increase the quality of their work and their lives.

For example, in an outstanding independent school, the faculty members focused on increasing their students' willingness to take risks when writing and to treat peers with more respect. In a rural school in the Midwest, teachers were eager to expand their students' openness to artistic and aesthetic experience. In many of our nation's classrooms, fundamental literacy skills are identified as a priority so learners can have access to all areas of the curriculum.

The Empty Chair

For many years now, whenever I work with a school or district, we begin the workshop or meeting by placing an empty chair in clear view of all participants. We envision that a student sits in that chair. We even use the first name of an actual child who attends the school—perhaps it's Johnny, Maria, Abdul, Megan, Tyler, or Janice. All our work that day must focus on Johnny, and all comments and questions are welcomed as long as they are in his best interest. We may disagree about what is in his best interest, but we do not lose the student as our perspective. Success really does come down to the critical point whereby we are working for specific learners in specific places to meet their specific needs. As Ouchi (2003, p. 159) of UCLA's Anderson Graduate School of Management states:

> Almost every expert who has studied successful schools says that they are learning communities where everyone is on the same page. The adults involved in the school—meaning the parents and teachers—must share the same vision of what the school should be.

A community is a group of individuals who have come together around a common goal, the unique definition of what kind of school they want to have. It will always be different for each school, as it should be, but it will always focus on the welfare of the children.

An Advance Team: Carrying Out Mapping R&D

Schools that have sustained this successful work—those in which teachers appear to be engaged in the review process and where results for learners are significant—began their mapping efforts with an advance cadre of research and development (R&D). This cadre carries out the necessary research to develop a plan of action. Composed of teachers and administrators from each site (or division, if working on the independent school level), the cadre members commence the initial investigative part of the process. The following four steps for crafting the prologue will help advance leadership planners launch a curriculum mapping initiative. References to upcoming chapters in this book are highlighted as they pertain to supporting each step.

Step 1: Focus on Research That Commences the Prologue

The ultimate goal of the prologue is to research external and internal data leading to recommendations about planning and instituting the mapping process. Researchers are concerned with all of the factors that have a direct effect on curriculum, assessment, and instruction. Eventually, they will make specific site-based recommendations about beginning and sustaining the mapping process. A large district may want to undertake mapping, but the power of the work is at the site. The district level can assist in orchestrating, coordinating, and supporting mapping work, but mapping succeeds best if the special characteristics and needs of each site are respected.

External data include becoming familiar with the mapping process and visiting and interviewing schools that have incorporated mapping into their decision-making process. Reading pertinent articles or books, viewing videos, and attending conferences and training on mapping and alignment are part of initial scouting. The review of internal data starts with unpacking assessment data about learners, considering students' demographic data, ascertaining each teacher's readiness to map, reflecting on the staff's past successful development efforts, and sketching out possible time frames for planning the workshops. The planning team should ask these questions:

• What are the optimum conditions for success?

• Who should meet with whom to start our work?

• What types of venues make sense for the readiness level of our staff members?

• What technology formats are available or could become available?

Mapping is a venture that requires preparedness through R&D. Taking the time to invest in the intellectual capital of the leadership cadre will reap dividends in the years ahead when virtually all teachers will be entering and reviewing their mapping data.

In 1991, Dr. Ann Johnson and her team of bright, motivated, and humorous teachers from Ankeny, Iowa, packed a van and traveled from the plains to the mountains of Colorado to attend an ASCD workshop. Dr. Johnson wanted her group to know more and ask more about mapping, and she wanted the "gel" that traveling can bring. With nuance, depth, and power, her group has continued to work and build their mapping program into this new century. Located in the greater Des Moines area, Ankeny has the blend of suburb and rural community that is prevalent throughout the heartland of the United States. What is remarkable about this district is the sustained growth it has demonstrated. Dr. Johnson prepared her group through reading, conferences, videos, interviews, site visits, and planning. The humor was always there when needed. Chapter 4 of this book reflects the power of the prologue that was part of the Ankeny planning experience. It is fair to say that the schools in Ankeny could not have had their long-term success while using the mapping process among learners if the teachers had jumped into mapping cold.

The active professional development consortium, Co-Nect, which is based in Cambridge, Massachusetts, recommends that formal surveys of staff members and students can prove most helpful when asking about their knowledge and interest in mapping. Through tallying responses, the advance leadership team can bring even more power to the planning process

(Friedberg & Fedolfi, 2001, p. 32). From the outset, input from all parties and from local demographic data is a fundamental part of internal research.

Another internal consideration is the professional expertise of staff members. Successful workshops on mapping basics should correspond to the faculty's background in assessment, curriculum design, and familiarity with standards. Schools in which the faculty's readiness in those areas is strong will tend to work much faster than schools whose faculties lack such experience.

Step 2: Draft an Action Plan

The advance team's investigations lead to their drafting an action plan that describes a sensible series of actions to implement mapping. Incremental steps translate into a plan for the next few months, six months, one year, or even three years. There is no question that plans change, but it is critical to have a plan to react to in the beginning of the mapping process. In fact, many schools "map the mapping process." (See Appendix 4 for an example of this.)

The need to align classroom work with standards has been a driving force behind the curriculum mapping process. A strong and compelling argument can be made for the power of integrating standards into the maps with a direct eye to student assessment. Research from the Ohio State Administrative Council report, *A Case Study of Key Effective Practices in Ohio's Improved School Districts*

(Ohio State Department of Education, 2001), indicates that mapping curriculum alignment was the most commonly identified strategy for improving student performance.

Analyzing the Social and Structural Realities of Staff Development at the Site. Whether private or public, the leadership cadre should play analytical hardball to determine the best way to carry out a mapping plan. No two schools are alike, and the advance-planning team should think carefully about the dynamics of a school faculty. The team would do well to get out of the box and invent ways of pulling members of the school together for optimum results. Too often, we run on habit, and, too often, staff development falls prey to the very ruts it purports to avoid.

In short, rather than simply jumping to the usual workshop mode to introduce mapping, the advance team should consider the types of initiatives that have been well received in the past. The team should look not only at the subject matter, but also at its organization and the venue used to introduce the subject matter. Consider asking, "What types of staff development opportunities exist?" and "Can we rethink the way we use those?" Video conferencing, work sessions, computer labs, study groups, interviews, and external conferences are venues to consider. Chapter 10 addresses "differentiated staff development" not only as a concept for carrying out mapping, but also as a kind

of staff development that is long overdue in our plans for improvement. An action plan should match the type of venue with a corresponding grouping of staff members.

We can avoid ruts through thoughtful planning. For example, many school districts have several event days for professional development when students are not in school. On those days, planning teams for mapping can stay in their schools instead of attending a keynote address with other teachers in a high school auditorium. Teachers who are new to the mapping process might spend their day entering data on maps and getting feedback from their technology department. More advanced groups might have teachers working in various configurations, reviewing maps and making alterations based on the needs of their students.

On more than one occasion, I have served as a coach, rather than as a featured speaker, where teachers on wireless laptops sit in groups and read maps in relation to their students' performance data. The decisions that follow are informed, immediate, and lasting. Even in schools lacking widespread access to computers, teachers can eventually enter their paper and pencil findings into an electronic database. Some schools have used faculty meetings or have changed the random nature of workshops into mapping work sessions. The key was that the time had already been set aside for professional development; it was simply used more effectively.

Documenting the Curriculum Mapping Process. Documenting, or "mapping," the mapping process is the logical outgrowth of advance research. It is logical then to have the prologue group document and map "their planning experience" in the initial stages. Everyone in the school or the district will eventually be involved in mapping, and they should know from the outset what is going on and how the process is unfolding in real time.

To demonstrate this point, consider the example of schools in North Carolina's District Five. In Chapter 2, Valerie Truesdale, Claire Thompson, and Michael Lucas underscore the need to make the work at hand clear and public and to anchor the work in the calendar—a hallmark of curriculum mapping. The power of mapping is its explicitness, particularly at the building, or school, level. All professionals in the schools and districts involved should know about the research. They should know that follow-up is necessary to sustain the work. These maps of the mapping process essentially display the action plans of the prologue planners, which is in contrast to the "covert activity" that has occurred when districts allow a well-intentioned committee to devise a plan that only they really understand or even know about. Teachers are right to ask, "How do we know that this new initiative is going to last and that there will be follow-up?" A genuine way

to reassure constituents is for planners to draw up actions on a calendar, with designated players assigned to carry out the actions.

Some unique issues correspond to the nature of different school settings, such as alternative and independent schools. In Chapter 8, Joseph Lachowicz describes mapping programs in alternative education settings. Working in 11 distinctive alternative program settings in his county in Pennsylvania, his team planned intricate and specific ways for teams to work within and among these district settings to collect and adapt curriculum maps for their students.

Independent schools are not bound to state standards. They are, however, directly accountable to parents and the marketplace. It is tempting in an independent school environment to let "independence run wild," with each teacher left alone to make curriculum decisions (National Association of Independent Schools, 2001). Mapping, therefore, has become a critical force in independent school education, often satisfying accreditation needs. More important, it allows for smoother transitions from year to year and provides a way to document some of the great teaching that occurs in independent schools. Stephen O'Neil's work, described in Chapter 5, reflects the path that private school faculty members might consider in curriculum mapping.

Step 3: Choose the Technology Template for Curriculum and Assessment Mapping

One of the most critical decisions the planning team makes is selecting a common computerized format for entering data on curriculum maps. Having a template in place *before* staff members are asked to enter their information saves hours of time and frustration. Many districts ask teachers to handwrite their mapping drafts—obviously a 19th-century approach to communication that does not bode well for the future. Computer databases allow teachers to edit with ease and to share their changes immediately.

The choice for a template should be consistent within all schools in a district so that all faculty members can easily read maps developed at other schools. Although the structure of classroom time between a high school and elementary school differs, teachers in both types of schools set up curriculum based on content, skill, and assessment. Consider an architectural analogy. Thousands and thousands of building styles exist throughout the world, yet any two architects can read each other's blueprints. In that same spirit, teachers can design countless approaches to the curriculum and the classroom, yet through mapping they can read each other's plans with ease.

While most districts design their own template using a database that is familiar to all the players, some districts and schools purchase Internet-based mapping programs

or software that have been developed commercially. The case studies in this book reflect both approaches: schools that have developed their own programs and those that have purchased Internet services.

It is important during prologue planning to investigate and research the differences between Intranet (internal between sites in a district) and Internet programs. Internet-based programs make communication possible from any location—home, public, or school—where there is access. Therefore, a classroom teacher can work at home and not be confined to working only on an Intranet environment at school.

In Chapter 7, Bena Kallick and James Wilson discuss those critical choices. They believe that electronic mapping presents the opportunity to create new knowledge that can help learning organizations make more intelligent choices for students. The actual format can expand the functions and options for educators. Butcher paper and index cards simply do not provide for sustained, engaging, and responsive communication. In addition, paper and cards also create storage problems.

Step 4: Plant Seeds to Ensure That Mapping Becomes Part of the Institution

As older ways of making decisions are eventually replaced (see Chapter 10), planners should integrate mapping into the fabric of the school program in the following ways:

• Identify potential places in the school-year calendar where existing staff development time could be used to carry out mapping tasks.

• Identify key people to help support the work in each school on the basis of their attitude and instructional power.

• Identify a specific time frame for beginning the critical first year of the mapping project.

• Create meaningful roles for participants.

• Locate research sources, such as books, articles, studies, videotapes, Web sites, and Web-based courses on mapping (see Curriculum Mapping Resources, pp. 170–171).

• Locate human resources involved in mapping: districts that have carried out mapping projects, individual consultants, staff developers from regional service centers, national organizations, workshops, institutes, and conferences.

This book provides specific examples and case studies that describe how various schools and school districts addressed those initial decisions.

When a school has not selected an advance-planning group to lead mapping preparation, there is the potential for trouble. If only one person leads the way, others can become defensive and resistant. For example, a principal or assistant superintendent may become *inspired* by a workshop. As a result, staff members might react with a "duck and cover" mentality. Their reaction might be, "Oh-oh, Dr. Smith just came back from a conference and is *enlightened* again." Making mapping work requires patience, persistence, and knowledge. Curriculum mapping is predicated on the community of a school coming to the table and looking at cumulative practices. Therefore, it is critical that a subset of that community conducts active advance R&D. Whether school leaders come or go, a stable database remains. Mapping should not be based on a personality or the charisma factor.

After the Prologue, No Epilogue

Mapping requires that all teachers create maps of their own practice. Each student's journey will ultimately be reflected in the maps. The combination of student performance data viewed in light of the K–12 curriculum path provides the big picture we need to zoom into each classroom and make critical revisions. As experienced teachers retire, they can pass on the legacy of their maps and their plans. Indeed, mapping is a way of electronically passing the torch.

As the advance-planning team moves into operation and mapping begins, some basic questions continue to be addressed:

• What are the optimum conditions to sustain our mapping work?

• Who should meet with whom to examine our mapping data in both the short term and the long term?

• What venues should we create to provide opportunities for ongoing review of K–12 curriculum and assessment?

• How can we use our technology to expand curriculum possibilities, search our database, and communicate with our education community?

Unlike the prologue analogy that is useful in getting started with mapping, there is no epilogue once the process begins. The work of curriculum mapping never ends. Knowledge will continue. Student populations will change. The strength of curriculum mapping is its ability to provide a living document that can respond to our learners' futures.

Use of Curriculum Mapping to Build a Learning Community

Valerie Truesdale, Claire Thompson, and Michael Lucas

Learning communities don't just magically appear. They must be built with a vision for how individual educators can support the achievement of each student through an articulated, seamless curriculum. Schools in District Five of Lexington and Richland Counties, a district close to the capital city of Columbia, South Carolina, are building their learning community using the tools provided in curriculum mapping. The history of the district shows how curriculum mapping was used to build a cohesive learning community. This chapter describes the support beams, processes, professional development, critical elements, obstacles, map development, and ways the process was sustained. The key points of the blueprint, presented as a closing summary, will remind readers of how important mapping tools can be in building a collaborative learning community through the development of a cohesive curriculum.

History of the District

School District Five is composed of nineteen schools that serve almost 16,000 students from child development through adult education. District schools are located in three distinct communities: Irmo, Chapin, and Dutch Fork. Historically, the communities were relatively homogenous in socioeconomic and demographic aspects. Equal resources have been provided for all schools, and excellence was expected and achieved. Schools in District Five led the state on all standardized measures of achievement for many years. More than 90 percent of students have attended college, and rarely did a student fail the state's high school exit exam.

In recent years, however, District Five has seen dramatic demographic shifts. A housing project in nearby urban Columbia closed, and many residents relocated to suburban areas, including the area served by the district. In addition, land development in one of the high school attendance zones pulled upper-middle-class families into another high school's attendance zone. Those population shifts produced more heterogeneous schools and resulted in different challenges. One school moved from 15 percent of the students receiving free and reduced-price lunches to more than 50 percent in a few years. Another school experienced a 35 percent transience rate, when more than one-third of the school's children who participated in state testing in the spring had not been enrolled the previous August.

Such changes challenged district leaders to address new curricular and instructional issues to ensure that high expectations and student achievement remained strong. District leaders searched for solutions and found that curriculum mapping provided useful tools to help build a strong, cohesive learning community. We can compare the tools of curriculum mapping to those on a worker's tool belt (see Figure 2.1)—a useful metaphor that focused the district's work. For instance, curriculum mapping is like a tool belt because it contains or holds information

about what a teacher *really* teaches:

- The *belt* is the calendar that organizes the tools.
- The *belt buckle* allows for adjustable pacing throughout the school year.
- The content *hammers* in the standards—the *nails*.
- The mapping tool *drills* in essential questions for authentic probing and learning.
- The *pliers* (skills) hold the content, standards, and assessments together.
- The *screwdriver* turns content into knowledge.
- The *measuring tape* can be used to assess student buildings (products).

Factors Leading to Curriculum Mapping

In 1994, the community adopted a strategic plan that called for "world-class standards." In 1995, teachers developed those standards, reaching a districtwide consensus about what students should know and be able to do in each content area. As part of that two-year staff development initiative, instructional leaders noticed some serious disconnects between what was expected of students and what they were taught. When teachers asked questions such as, "Do all students write research papers in high school?" and "When do we ensure that skills in an area are taught?" the answer was, "It depends." What a student was taught depended completely on the student's teacher. Each teacher

Fig. 2.1   Curriculum Mapping: A Tool Belt for Teachers

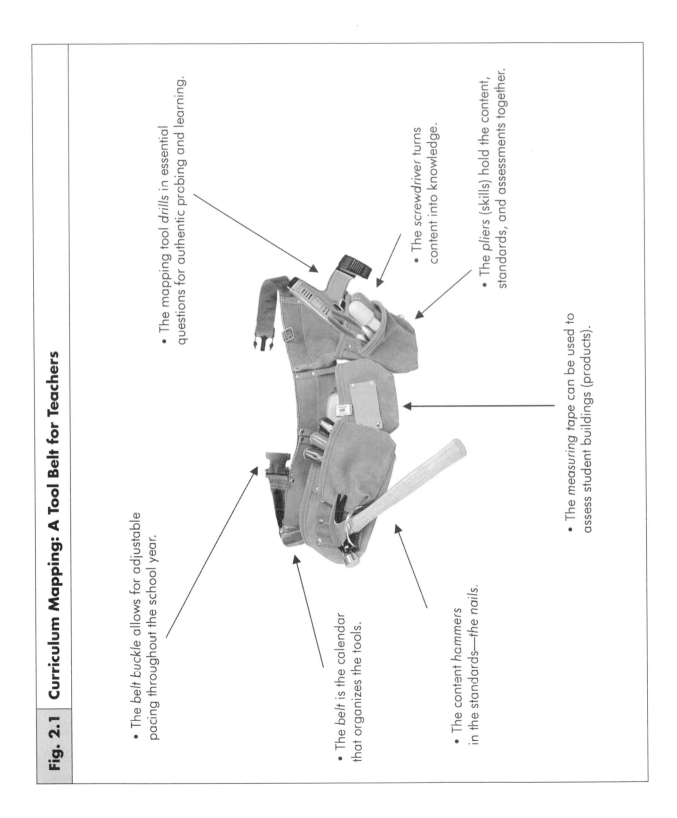

- The *belt buckle* allows for adjustable pacing throughout the school year.

- The mapping tool *drills* in essential questions for authentic probing and learning.

- The *screwdriver* turns content into knowledge.

- The *pliers* (skills) hold the content, standards, and assessments together.

- The *belt* is the calendar that organizes the tools.

- The content *hammers* in the standards—the nails.

- The *measuring tape* can be used to assess student buildings (products).

decided which standards to address and what experiences to provide. Therefore, the quality of each student's learning depended entirely on what a teacher decided to emphasize. The lack of horizontal consistency across schools and vertical continuity within schools created a major barrier to quality. In addition, once teachers in School District Five developed district standards and aligned them to state standards, the volume of standards was immense. In the 7th and 8th grades alone, more than 1,000 standards existed in the core subject areas! Instructional leaders surmised that with the volume of standards to address, decisions regarding what was taught should not be an "it depends" issue. The district needed a plan for building a strong, cohesive curriculum.

Although School District Five adopted high academic standards and the most rigorous curriculum materials available, some teachers did not embrace the district's curriculum, claiming that students were not able to do the work. As both the volume of standards and the demographic differences grew, a sense of isolation also emerged among teachers and administrators. Educators needed to connect with colleagues as they struggled to change teaching practices so they could meet more comprehensive standards. Teams of teachers were challenged to think through the mind of a child rather than with the child in mind. In other words, they were asked to envision learning opportunities as if they were individual children moving from kindergarten to 12th grade in the

district. What experiences would students have? What would connect learning for them? The resulting plan had to include specifics so that educators could examine the total structure and establish a strong community of learning.

Support Beams: The Leadership Roles

Instructional leaders recognized that a process that brings individuals together to reflect and share information must support the learning community across diverse schools within a school district. For many years, a hallmark of School District Five had been instructional leadership provided by teacher and administrator teams. Teachers, working side-by-side with administrators, made decisions that affected student learning. Curriculum mapping had to support this process so that teachers' leadership roles remained intact. One way educators have retained this collaboration is with leadership teams. Teachers and administrators representing all grade levels and all schools meet monthly to make decisions regarding teaching and learning across the entire district. These leadership teams provide instructional leadership by involving stakeholders and moving all schools as a unit toward their goals.

By using a building metaphor, instructional leaders decided the district needed support beams from school to school to build a new sense of community. One of the support beams was consistent expectations undergirded by sufficient resources to meet the needs of schools with more challenges. A second support beam was guidance for teachers in managing an overwhelming curriculum. A third was greater connection among content areas so students could see the relevance of lessons.

To construct the support beams, leaders needed to foster a sense of cohesion among teachers, and teachers needed tools for sharing information quickly with one another. To connect the beams, smoother transitions were needed at critical junctures, such as elementary school to middle school and middle school to high school. To cement skills at benchmark grades and to increase student comprehension, educators believed a deeper commitment to teaching reading in all content areas was critical. The leaders saw curriculum mapping as a tool to address those needs, because it built a renewed sense of community by using instructional reflection and professional collaboration.

Process of Implementing Curriculum Mapping

Continuing the construction metaphor, the leaders realized that a new structure could not be built without plans (a blueprint) and a vision of what the structure (architecture) would look like. The district needed to identify a vision for the community, develop research sites, engage the architects, clear the land, establish a foundation, and use tools to construct the community. When the leaders learned about Dr. Heidi Hayes Jacobs's research in curriculum mapping, they realized that mapping held promise as a unifier around which to build a renewed sense of community. After considerable research through professional journals, conferences sponsored by the Association for Supervision and Curriculum Development (ASCD), and telephone interviews with other district leaders, such as in Ankeny, Iowa, the District Five leaders decided to study the feasibility of implementing curriculum mapping. Thus, a vision was created.

In School District Five, involvement of stakeholders is a standard for every initiative. The leaders recruited two highly skilled principals, Michael Lucas (secondary level) and Claire Thompson (elementary level), to mastermind a blueprint for building the learning community. In 1999–2000, the district selected 62 teachers, representing various grades, subject areas, and schools, who would work with Lucas and Thompson in a graduate-level course to study the feasibility of implementing curriculum mapping. Using ASCD tapes and books written by Dr. Jacobs (see Curriculum Mapping Resources and Bibliography, pp. 170–173), course participants learned about and tried curriculum mapping techniques in their classrooms. The teachers studied various designs for District Five maps. They interviewed experts to refine their design. In a workshop with the class in January 2000, Dr. Jacobs provided her strong help with the design.

The graduate course participants became the chief architects of the community-building initiative. They tested the ground to see if it was ready to build on by using mapping in their own classrooms. They sought resources to support an articulated curriculum. Course participants understood clearly that if they determined the ground was not ready, the district would not use curriculum mapping. As architects, they could decide to use different tools. At the end of the graduate course, however, the architects decided to move forward with building the community in all schools using curriculum mapping as the major tool. In fact, they decided to build a community across all schools rather than implement mapping in only a few schools as a pilot project. They recognized that with more than 1,200 teachers, this initiative would be no small undertaking. The architects carefully designed the process, identified the tools needed, and pledged a three-year commitment to the building process. The graduate course participants used the template developed in *Mapping the Big Picture: Integrating Curriculum and Assessment K–12.* (Jacobs, 1997a) shown in Figure 2.2. More than 1,200 teachers used this to record their initial maps; an example from an actual school is shown in Figure 2.3.

Professional Development to Establish a Foundation

As good architects do, the graduate course participants identified the tools needed to teach more than 1,200 teachers about curriculum mapping. To lay the foundation, the course participants served as workshop leaders on staff development days during the 2000–2001 school year. They developed PowerPoint presentations and shared the

Fig. 2.2	Standard Template for Initial Curriculum Maps			
	August	**September**	**October**	**November**
Content				
Skill				
Assessment				
Technology				
Other/Essential Questions				

Source: Jacobs (1997a).

Fig. 2.3	**Example of Curriculum Map Using Modified Standard Template**

Teacher: *Karl Hudson*   **Grade:** *8/Social Studies*   **School:** *District Five Middle School*

	August	**September**
Essential Questions	• How does the geography of SC and the US affect the settlement of the country? • Does geography affect industrial development?	• How were the Native Americans changed by their interaction with the early explorers? • How did the Protestant Reformation influence the Exploration Period?
Content	• Geography (US & SC) • State symbols	• Native Americans • Early exploration
Skills/ Benchmarks	• 8.2.1: Discuss influence of physical geography on SC history. • 8.8.1: Make and use maps of SC and US. • 8.8.2: Describe and locate physical characteristics. • 8.8.3: Explain how people interacted with the physical environment in SC and US.	• 8.2.2: Discuss life in the Americas before arrival of Europeans and Africans. • 8.8.3: Describe how people inter-acted with their environment—SC and US. • 8.8.4: Explain patterns and types of migrations.
Assessments	• Maps • Quiz • Major test on SC and US geography • Brochure—Region Project • "Journey Through SCIG"	• Native American stories and myths • Explorers Chart • Picture from definitions • Video notes • Essay—*Hope for the Flowers* • Explorer PowerPoint
Activities (Required)	• "Who Am I?" sheets • Ball-Toss Name Game • Textbook scavenger hunts (US & SC) • US physical and climate maps, SC physical map • Pictures from definitions • States Game—puzzle pieces on overhead • Intro to laptops—"Journey Through SCIG" • Brochure—Region Project	• Internet research site • Major test—Native Americans • Writing a myth • Pictures from definitions • Video—"In Search of the First Americans" • Teen *Newsweek* • Cards to soldiers in Afghanistan • Read *Hope for the Flowers* • Begin research on Explorer PowerPoint
Miscellaneous Notations (Optional)		
Technology (Optional)	• SC video—"Smiling Faces, Beautiful Faces" • Laptops—SCIG • Brochure—Region Word Document	• Video—"In Search of Native Americans" • Explorer PowerPoint Project

Source: School District Five of Lexington and Richland Counties, South Carolina.

curriculum maps they developed during the graduate course. All District Five teachers received templates on diskettes, along with notebooks that included essential information on mapping and the K–12 curriculum standards for their area of teaching. Course participants also trained building-level administrators and department leaders in the use of mapping tools and taught peer-coaching skills to instructional leaders. Curriculum mapping (CM) coaches were in every school. These CM coaches participated in a second graduate course during the 2000–2001 school year to develop tools that would further refine the building process. Leaders of this second graduate course were Harriet Wilson, an elementary principal, and Beth Moore, the district's teacher of the year.

Building a cohesive community for a strong district curriculum extended even further. Each school began its own individual building process by choosing content areas to map. In August 2000, each elementary school began mapping one core content area—math or science. All teachers in grades 6–12 mapped at least one of their courses. Teachers of related areas mapped at least one course as well. Guidance counselors and media specialists also developed a map of their classroom teaching activities for the year. Special education, physical education, and other content-area teachers developed specialized maps, some of which covered multiple years to fit the discipline.

On staff development days during the school year, coaches facilitated mixed-group and like-group review sessions to refine maps. In May 2001, each teacher submitted at least one reviewed and revised map for a collective districtwide review during Summer Institute, which is a week-long activity held in June for highly motivated teachers who meet to work on curriculum issues. Between 120 and 200 teachers learn and work together each summer, earning graduate or recertification credit. Summer Institute for 2001 was dedicated to reviewing initial maps to strengthen the foundation of the renewed community of adult learners.

To support the foundation, district leaders identified policies and practices that could be streamlined to validate the use of the tools of curriculum mapping. Administrators revised the teacher evaluation system to accommodate curriculum maps. The requirement for first-year teachers to submit long-range plans was changed; instead, they were to develop projected curriculum maps. The district provided maps developed by exemplary teachers to guide new teachers as they planned their year. District-level content coordinators were expected to ask for maps when they observed in classrooms and were to provide targeted feedback to teachers about how their teaching and assessments aligned with state and district standards. Curriculum maps from regular education teachers were shared with special education teachers to forge new connections. Resource teachers added their curriculum to the maps of the regular education teachers to help students make connections between learning in the resource room and learning in the regular classroom.

At some schools, the foundation was built easily, because the soil had been tilled and the pilings were put in place without much resistance. Leaders in those buildings were deeply committed to the process and were well aware of how to use the tools in their toolbox. Their tools included the skills of teachers and leaders to adapt to change and the decision-making processes already in place.

Teachers in those schools were accustomed to working in collegial teams and had been empowered to make curriculum revisions in a climate of acceptance for their professionalism. The leader was willing to pick up a hammer and to work alongside the teachers in developing, reviewing, and revising the structures. Both leaders and teachers valued process and dialogue as tools to improve instruction. Mapping was seen as a way to shape a dialogue, rather than as a new or different approach to teaching. The tools already in place in those schools were augmented by curriculum mapping tools that teachers used to model the building process on the new site—a different way of planning for improvement of instruction. Leaders used the information gained from working side-by-side with teachers to design staff development sessions that were then based on opportunities identified in the curriculum maps.

At some schools, the curriculum mapping process was met with initial resistance. The tools, however, brought teachers together in both mixed- and like-group reviews, resulting in some surprises in content. As coaching became more sophisticated, instructional leaders in the schools became more diligent in asking questions centered on the maps, and the building tools began to be used more and more. Coaches and content coordinators met monthly to share building challenges and to suggest approaches for making the building process more successful. Meetings of CM coaches also provided feedback on progress within each school and guided the work and direction of the entire district.

Blueprint for the Foundation: Identifying Critical Elements

Instructional leaders found that the following factors contributed to a successful foundation:

• *Size of the site (school):* Fewer teachers equaled greater opportunities for sharing in mixed- and like-group reviews. Thus, in larger schools, breaking dialogues into smaller groups proved helpful.

• *Size of the community:* Three distinct communities exist in the district, each consisting of a high school with its feeder schools. In the smallest of the three communities, with only four schools, collaboration of K–12 curriculum was easier for planning reviews across grade levels. In the larger feeder systems, breaking the K–12 dialogues into smaller groups was helpful. For example, when four elementary schools, one middle school, and one large high school met for mixed- and like-group reviews of K–12, scheduling dialogues at three locations worked better than organizing hundred of teachers in one place.

• *Depth of the soil:* The degree to which there was deep commitment to enhancing teaching and learning practices among instructional leaders within a building was factored into the use of curriculum mapping as a tool for collegial dialogue. When the leaders lacked such commitment, leadership from the district was needed to build school-level capacity for change.

• *Skill of the builders:* Once the architects (participants in the first graduate course) outlined a process for building an overall plan for a community, the skill of the site leaders to take the overall plan and to articulate it into a site plan by putting in structures to support the foundation made a difference in acceptance. A weak building process meant either building leaders had a lukewarm commitment to the process or leaders lacked knowledge in how to build a foundation for change. Leaders held staff development sessions on managing change and channeling resistance in productive ways.

System to Uncover the Rocks: Addressing Obstacles

In building a community, architects must identify obstacles so that a firm foundation can be built. However, when rocks are just below the surface, construction can be delayed. The same is true in the process of curriculum mapping. Some schools already had a firm foundation of sharing teaching and learning strategies, and, therefore, the building process was systematic and challenging, but not overwhelming. In some schools, however, rocks of resistance were just below the surface. The process of curriculum mapping and sharing across schools highlighted teachers who either were not following the adopted district curriculum or were not teaching to state and district standards. In some schools, leaders had not addressed the resistance of a few teachers to believe that all children can learn at high levels.

When construction crews hit rock, the rock has to be extracted. Removing rock (extracting old attitudes) and bringing in new dirt (introducing new information about teaching and learning) were necessary before some schools could begin to lay the foundation for curriculum mapping. The district provided school leaders with the tools needed to manage the resistance and support teachers as they stretched themselves and their students. In some cases, individuals were given intensive training so they could acquire the necessary skills to accomplish the task.

Framework: Developing Maps

Using the tools that had been developed required diligent attention to detail. CM coaches and the instructional team (principals, assistant principals, and department or grade-level leaders) served as site chiefs to lead the building project in each school. Administrators provided assistance to teachers to help make the process align with the focus of the district or school. Teachers used forms like the one shown in Figure 2.4 to help them align their work with the focus of the school district and their individual schools.

Educators with extensive knowledge of process crafted certain specialized aspects within each school. For example, in one high school, a CM coach focused on forging a dialogue between the English and social studies teachers as they examined their maps for humanities courses. The coach used her knowledge of process and curriculum to craft mixed- and like-group reviews, yielding greater understanding of the content, skills, and assessments needed to improve learning for the students. In another situation, district content coordinators provided specialized expertise to coach teachers in strengthening their maps to appropriately align skills and assessments. Other examples include CM coaches and instructional leaders helping teachers identify gaps and overlaps in their K–12 curriculums and proposing ways to improve experiences for students, plus coaches encouraging educators to think of nontraditional ways to teach and assess students. In each case, coaches and leaders identified risk takers, supported them, and recognized their willingness to share their ideas. Without the risk takers, every building in the mapping community would be the same, more like cookie-cutter houses than homes with individual personalities. Maps began to naturally evolve and to reflect similarities within schools; however, throughout the process, mapping coaches emphasized the importance of creativity and individuality.

A Look at Finishing Touches: Sustaining the Process

To sustain the sense of building a community, the mapping process needed strong buttresses, which were provided through various means, to identify areas needing attention within individual schools and throughout the school system. In District Five, leadership teams of content teachers have been meeting monthly to set the direction for curriculum and instructional issues. One buttress provided mapping support as leadership teams opened each meeting by updating development of curriculum maps. Another buttress provided mixed- and like-group reviews that focus on obvious overlaps that the schools could address: for example, in one elementary school, two different grades were teaching the metamorphosis of the butterfly; school-level negotiations yielded a revised insect unit for 4th grade.

Fig. 2.4	Sample Expectations for Departments or Grade Levels			
Department or Grade:				
Yes	**No**	**In Process**	**Goal**	
			1. Participate in initial training session.	
			2. Conduct department session to discuss curriculum mapping terminology and to develop some consistency in definitions: (a) content, (b) skill, (c) assessment, (d) technology, and (e) essential questions.	
			3. Ensure that a departmental list of maps will be developed in the department or grade so that all preparations are represented in the interdisciplinary reviews.	
			4. Have department members participate in follow-up training session.	
			5. Collect copies of first draft, and submit a copy to assistant principal for instruction.	
			6. Collect revised first draft and skeleton maps, and submit a copy.	
			7. Collect assessment items for each grading period (for use in looking at assessment component of map).	
			8. Ensure that departments or grade levels periodically review maps during monthly meetings to make sure that (a) essential questions focus instruction, (b) content is appropriate, (c) skills are aligned with content, and (d) assessments are appropriate and aligned with skills. (Assessments may include tests but should also include alternative assessment such as projects and performance tasks.)	
			9. Have department members work together to identify any gaps and repetitions in the curriculum and to resolve gaps or repetitions.	
			10. Have department members participate in school-wide interdisciplinary teams to examine or resolve gaps and repetitions in the curriculum.	
			11. Make final copies of all maps when they are completed, and turn them in to the principal.	

Leaders learned to trust the process to bring the "a-ha" to teachers (perhaps serving as electricians who turn on lighting in the community). Individual school teams worked through initial refinements. Decisions then were fortified by the buttresses that gave specific data about the need for improvement through the curriculum maps.

Another buttress for the mapping process was provided in the summer during professional development institutes, when educators reviewed thousands of maps and discovered a need to make systemwide changes in curriculum. Although gaps and overlaps in content and assessments were easier to identify than skill gaps, once teachers became familiar with the systemic review process, areas needing attention became apparent. Teachers were familiar with the process of mixed- and like-group reviews at the school level and, therefore, found district-level reviews manageable. Teams of trainers addressed the districtwide and building-level professional development offerings for the next year that had been designed around the systemic gaps and overlaps identified in the Summer Institute.

Another buttress provided the development of curriculum materials and instructional processes. It provided teacher support materials that had been based on needs identified from maps. A review of math maps indicated the need for support in math skills in the upper elementary grades. As a result, teams of teachers developed curriculum materials during the summer months to share with their colleagues in the fall. In addition, a review of social studies maps across K–12 revealed that students were being taught about the Holocaust four different times but rarely learned about the Gulf War. Teachers then adjusted the curriculum maps. Teachers also determined that the five-paragraph essay was overused as an assessment, so they circulated examples of other assessment tools among teachers and instructional leaders.

The maps revealed as a weakness the lack of articulated study skills across grades. High school teachers expected students to outline and take notes, but K–8 maps showed no evidence of explicit teaching of study skills. A task force developed standards for study skills for grades 3–12 and shared them with teachers on staff development days.

Reviewing maps indicated a need to differentiate instruction for students at varying levels of ability; thus, a team of trainers was sent to learn strategies for differentiating instruction. Reading maps across K–12 indicated that teachers expect a high level of reading comprehension for success in high school courses, yet there was little evidence that explicit reading strategies had been taught past 3rd grade. As a result, leaders launched a major initiative in building active literacy methods in all content areas.

Curriculum mapping is a work in progress in District Five. The structure is not complete, but the cornerstone of commitment in building collegial dialogue that focuses on teaching and learning has resulted in a districtwide community that honors reflection on instructional practice. The focus is leading to individual teachers' improvement of curriculum and instruction for all students.

Blueprint for Building a Community of Learners

Using our curriculum mapping work in District Five, we developed the following blueprint that we hope will be helpful to you in your work:

1. Explore ideas. Bring to the surface any needs for change.

2. Identify chief architects who will design improved ways of building student learning and of fostering collegiality among teachers across grade levels and schools.

3. Lay a firm foundation for change so that the architects' plans will be implemented on solid ground.

4. Identify rocks (obstacles) in the process of collegial growth, and take action to address challenges and resistance. Strength in instructional leadership is necessary to provide feedback to teachers and to stretch their creativity in designing ways to enhance dialogues among K–12 teachers.

5. Train craftspeople to support specialized needs, and provide time for them to work with school-level teams. Skilled coaches at each school and at the district level are key for modeling and supporting the collegial dialogues that are necessary for addressing gaps and overlaps.

6. Develop explicit plans. Staff development should be relevant, timely, and sustained. Equip your staff development leaders at both the school and the district levels with extensive tools for supporting school teams.

7. Follow through on details. Taking time to identify systemwide policies and practices that can be streamlined is important. For teachers to spend time developing curriculum maps, you need a corresponding reduction in other aspects of planning.

8. Update the community of learners constantly about the building process. Many initiatives are not successful in education because they are not sustained. Frequent updates in all meetings and constantly seeking ways to use maps as the hub of all discussions about teaching and learning will help institutionalize mapping as a daily tool.

9. Recognize that building a community of enhanced learning takes years. The progress will be slow but rewarding. Old habits of teaching in isolation must be replaced with shared ideas and with negotiated content and assessment. Sustained support is vital to successfully implement curriculum mapping as a tool for improving teaching of and learning by children.

Curriculum mapping has been a useful tool to bring about a synergy of professional expertise focused on instructional improvement in District Five. It has provided the tools to build a cohesive learning community with teachers as the chief architects and builders. Over several years, maps have become the hub for highlighting continual changes and refinements needed in the instructional program. Mapping has provided a process for collegial dialogue as it focuses on alignment of content, skills, assessments, and activities across 19 schools, with its ultimate goal of improving student achievement.

Development of a Consensus Map
Wrestling with Curriculum Consistency and Flexibility

Heidi Hayes Jacobs

Once the workshop begins and participants engage in learning about the nature of curriculum mapping, participants inevitably raise questions: "Shouldn't we eventually make a consensus map? Isn't that the point of mapping?" In other words, "Shouldn't all 3rd grade teachers be doing the same thing at the same time?" I would ask these questions instead: "What is in Johnny's best interest? When is consensus critical for Johnny's progress, and when is flexibility equally important?"

The 3rd grade teachers want to get together and make their consensus map *before* they have looked at any other grade levels. The high school social studies department wants to make decisions *before* examining not only the middle school social studies curriculum, but also any other subject area. Curriculum mapping provides a powerful opportunity to consider more subtle and nuanced considerations for learners as teachers wrestle with consensus.

A consensus curriculum map reflects the policy agreed on by a professional staff that targets those specific areas in each discipline that are to be addressed with consistency and flexibility in a school or a district. The result of this deliberation is an *essential* map.

The Latin for consensus is *consentiere*, meaning "to feel with; to feel the same." It is noteworthy that the Latin root does not mean to act the same way. It is important that teachers reach some professional agreements to ensure a meaningful journey for the learner. Their agreements can and should fulfill a range of approaches that do not encroach on classroom creativity, yet at the same time promise as smooth a journey as can be designed for the learner. This chapter probes the problems caused by hurried curriculum decision making and suggests policy guidelines for moving to an essential curriculum through the mapping process. The contention is that the tension between consistency and flexibility is a vital and dynamic basis for determining policies throughout each curriculum area. What should crystallize is the vision of a school in which communication and decisions are made directly in the children's best interest and are not based on old committee meeting habits.

Consensus Map Guidelines

It seems that curriculum decisions often are made too quickly. If we revisit the questions raised at the beginning of this chapter ("What is in Johnny's best interest? When is consensus critical for Johnny's progress, and when is flexibility equally important?"), it is clear that the key is thoughtful reflection.

A curious observation is the uniform way that committees review curriculum for each field of study. Too often authorities have a knee-jerk impulse to declare that "all curriculum areas will be the same." In fact, real and significant differences exist between fields of study. When discussing curriculum, we often use geopolitical metaphors, such as fields, worlds, areas, units, and boundaries. This usage is, in part, because there are rich and fascinating links between education and geopolitics (Jacobs, 1989). These differences highlight the perspectives that science, social studies, art, or math bring to the problems and topics under scrutiny. At the same time, when linked effectively, the curriculum areas can provide rich interdisciplinary experiences. When it comes to curriculum mapping, each discipline has its own unique characteristics. Therefore, the review of each discipline should take those characteristics into account. When planning interdisciplinary curriculum, multiple considerations come into play. As Rebecca Burns (2002, p. 64) points out:

> Many administrators and faculties fail to realize that implementing interdisciplinary teamed instruction affects all key components of schooling: organization and management, curriculum, instruction, assessment, and culture.

We must return to the child in the chair who is watching us work at the table or at the computer and must ask if our decisions will ultimately be in that child's best interest. Wrestling with a consensus map requires sophisticated thinking and debate among faculty members.

Mapping can help teachers in a number of ways as they provide the targeted consistency and yet still provide the flexibility that can prove equally as critical. Often, a department or group of grade-level teachers might agree to share the same essential question, or a set of essential questions, to focus their work. Schools in a district might vary methods, materials, and approaches to the same standards. To help provide a perspective for the district, for parents, and for individual teachers, schools can design common benchmark assessment tasks that reflect a specific standard (see Chapter 9). This approach allows each school to provide an integrated approach tailored to its own learners and, at the same time, to give a consistent focus to useful assessment tasks across the district.

Value of the Mixed-Group Review in Mapping

One of the most revealing and engaging steps in the mapping process is the mixed-group review, in which members of the faculty who do not regularly work together have the opportunity to do so. This interfacing creates a series of "jigsaw" review groups comprising faculty members who rarely get a chance to step out of the box and view the experience of students from new perspectives. For example, in an elementary school, kindergarten, 2nd grade, 4th grade, 5th grade, music, and special education teachers might form one group. Likewise, freshman social studies, senior English, business education, math, and studio art teachers might form a high school group. The purpose is to share observations targeted around a specific review task. Perhaps teachers are asked to review for repetitions or for gaps in either a specific subject or across a grade level.

Individually, teachers examine the maps and make their notations. The mixed-group review culls these observations and analyzes them.

Often in high school groups, participants question whether someone who does not teach a particular subject is qualified to read the map for another subject. Although a teacher may not have majored in or specialized in that area, he or she often brings a new perspective from an "outside" point of view. An analogy to book publishing might prove helpful here.

When an author submits a book to a publishing house, the editor often sends it out to two sources for feedback: one, a reader who is familiar with the subject and might find holes in the content; two, an excellent reader who is not an expert in the subject. The latter reader sees things that the former reader might miss. When someone is conversant on a topic, he or she may be too close to the material, read between the lines, and miss critical gaps.

The same holds true in the curriculum review process. Sometimes a science teacher reviewing math curriculum might see something that the math teacher might miss in terms of an opportunity or a need. Sometimes the 5th grade teacher will pick up on something the 1st grade teacher misses. Sometimes the physical education teacher might see a gap in the 7th grade health curriculum. We owe it to Johnny (in the chair) to share our viewpoints and to review the curriculum from many angles.

It is precisely after the mixed-group review that the discussion of a potential consensus map makes sense. Now the faculty members have a new and fresh perspective about their work. The various views from the jigsaw nature of the mixed group allow for more informed curriculum decisions. A genuine potential for a rewarding professional openness can follow from these discussions. When teachers and administrators examine the truth of their work with "warts and all," camaraderie emerges. Mapping does not purport to create an idealistic vision where all teachers agree, love one another, and gather around a campfire and sing "Curriculum Kumbaya." What it can develop is a sense of place, of respect, and of new grounds for discussion, disputes, and direction. Therefore, looking at the consensus question is best toward the end of the first year of mapping or when collected mapping data have been sufficiently examined both vertically and horizontally.

Dangers of Premature Consensus

There is an understandable tendency to put faculty members together in their usual patterns after collecting mapping data. This tendency, however, can cause potential problems for the learner. One might even say that this is why the learner often runs into trouble. The very gaps we wish to avoid are created when we do not look at the big picture.

For example, a high school social studies department might collectively make a decision about the format for research-oriented papers without looking at the format used in English or science. As a result, students might get mixed signals and become confused when working on a full range of academic subjects. Consider the decision made by 2nd grade teachers when they decided to teach a major unit with a theme on folk tales and fairy tales. The group not only failed to examine what occurred the previous year in 1st grade, but also never stepped back to look at the choices in language arts genre from a K–4 perspective. As it turned out, variations on folk tales and fairy tales were evident each year. Certainly some will argue that such stories have special meaning for young children, but when one thinks about the wide range of genre available and the fact that the choice was made in a grade-level vacuum, the decision is difficult to justify. Perhaps the children could use some nonfiction to build their reading skills as well.

If we return to the initial question raised in this chapter about consensus, we find choices about when to wrestle with consensus and flexibility and how to resolve such issues. The curriculum mapping process can provide solutions to those problems.

Process of Reaching a Curriculum Consensus Policy

As teachers and administrators examine the findings of a curriculum review, they have an opportunity to sort observations into two categories:

1. The level of difficulty and complexity in seeking a solution

a. Those that can be solved with relative ease in an immediate way

b. Those that require long-term research and development to create solutions

2. The tasks central to the mapping process (Jacobs, 1997a)

a. Filling in the gaps

b. Eliminating repetitions

c. Seeking potential areas for integration

d. Validating and integrating standards

e. Updating antiquated programs with timely curriculum

These two categories lead reviewers to focus on questions concerning consensus. In the course of resolving issues of repetition or gaps, sometimes we find that the question of consensus naturally emerges, thus alleviating the initial anxiety about whether "I am going to have to give up something I teach." When it is glaringly apparent that students will suffer because of a dearth of seamless curriculum planning, the discussion moves rapidly. In short, the maps are evidence that all reviewers see at the same time.

Tour of the Disciplines

One can find fascinating problems by touring the disciplines and considering the ways flexibility, or range, and consistency might vary in the review of specific subjects. At the time of this writing, schools in the United States are directly confronting standards that have, in fact, been organized into disciplines with few exceptions. Basic epistemology teaches us that each discipline has unique characteristics—in a sense, each has its own architecture. As Klein (1996, p. 38) points out, some disciplines are more permeable than others."

When a school is struggling with the issue of consensus, it is important to respect the distinctions and unique properties of each subject. It is not just a question of when to be consistent or flexible, but of how the subject will play out in the classroom. To set this point in concrete, consider the following perspectives when looking at the tension between consistency and flexibility. Questions toward building consensus developed before reviewing the map should reflect a sincere attempt to determine what is unique about the discipline to be examined. As you tour the landscape that follows about each discipline, clear and distinctive components in each are in **bold**. This "tour" aims to set a discussion into motion, rather than to suggest that the reader will agree with the policy points raised.

Math

Math is the most abstract discipline. It is based on numeric and conceptual relationships through nonverbal symbols. To assist learners in engaging with the language of mathematics, teachers are advised to be consistent with the **sequence** of math instruction over time. Teachers might be ill advised to teach fractions before students know how to divide or to teach measurement when students lack basic counting skills. It is not in the best interest of students for a teacher to randomly eliminate teaching multiplication and division for the sake of variety.

However, range in **pace** is equally critical for students in mathematics. The building blocks of mathematical thinking are requisite for more advanced conceptualization. If a student is not ready to move on, then the teacher must take time to assist that learner. As one teacher put it, "We cannot put the kids on the train for multiplication until they have the addition tickets."

A **flexible range of methods** for assisting learners does not alter the sequence. Students do not acquire mathematical understanding at the same pace. Therefore, a school might elect to have a consensus map that relies on a careful K–12 sequence over the years, but that maintains flexibility as to the rapidity of the pace and the range of assignments, methods, strategies, and experiences that children can be exposed to as they go from class to class.

Language Arts, World Language Instruction, and Literature

This area is strikingly different from mathematics. The question of consistency and range can be applied to (1) choice of **genre** studied, (2) specific **works** of literature, (3) specific **editing and revision** skills

when applying grammar, and (4) **theme**. In other words, five 4th grade teachers might agree with their colleagues when looking at the K–12 panorama that their 4th grade is a good time to introduce the genre of historical fiction. Consensus on the genre choice is accepted. The same team, however, could agree that there can be flexibility on the choice of specific literary works; not all teachers use the same textbook.

Yet, this flexibility proves problematic in other components of the language arts curriculum. It is difficult to argue that widely varying standards for editing their writing are helpful to learners. Here is a place where there is a need for great consistency. We do not want Johnny to get the message from one teacher that he needs to work on editing complete sentences in all his formal work, and then have him go to his second period class and find that the teacher does not care about the grammar "as long as the ideas are there."

Over the years, teachers may truly believe that they are introducing a *new* editing or revision skill. An examination of the maps, however, shows that the students have been introduced to the same skills five years in a row. We need to work diligently at spiraling language arts skills vertically as students advance in grade level. We also need to work at supporting those same skills and following through in all subject areas when students reach middle and high school.

The choice of literary works has powerful implications vertically. Sometimes a student will have studied a novel in an English class, only to find the same novel presented again two years later. When the student protests, the response is often a variation on "Yes, I know you studied the book in 6th grade, but you haven't had it with me. It will be a different book in 8th grade. You will learn so much more." Most students are not going to major in English. They are teenagers, and they resent the lack of variety. As a freshman boy put it in an interview, "Hey, if they can't take the time to do something different, why should I?"

English teachers frequently wrap the study of literary works around **themes**. Conceptual notions, such as **conflict**, **rites of passage**, or **survival**, serve students well in English classes as a perspective on learning. Yet themes too can become redundant. Maps allow teachers to share with one another the themes and corresponding works they present in a thoughtful review over time. Consensus in this case points to vertical articulation to avoid redundant themes.

World language teachers are often very clear and consistent over the years in the curriculum. They tend to have a spiraling approach to working with grammar, situational applications of vocabulary, and a range of assessments.

Social Studies

Social studies is often the most controversial, permeable, and fluid of disciplines. Decisions that are made often have social consequences and reflect social values. Whose history are we going to leave out? What cultural perspective should we take? Even in what appears to be a highly contained area like geography, the actual choice of map type reflects values. Mercator maps, which are perhaps the most widely used maps in U.S. classrooms, were developed in 1569 by a German named Gerardus Mercator to help sailors navigate. Not surprisingly, Germany is placed in the physical center of the map, causing remarkable distortions in proportion to other countries (for example, Greenland is larger than Africa, South America, or India). A Peters projection map gives an accurate representation of land size, but is startling to students when they see how different the "value" message is compared to the 16th century Mercator map that is still the touchstone for most students (and adults). In short, controversy trails social studies.

Questions for curriculum reviews during the mapping process often focus around questions specific to the various subdisciplines in social studies: geography, history, political science, and anthropology:

• **Geography.** Geography involves consensus on consistent timing as to when to introduce concepts and terms across the grade levels, a relatively straightforward task. Range, or flexibility, becomes a legitimate concern in terms of what types of assessment truly reflect understanding of geography concepts.

• **History.** History clearly requires a thorough consideration of the sequence and the selection of critical events, periods, people, and themes. It is advisable that a K–12 perspective be considered as students build a historical view while they move through school. There certainly might be a range of methods and approaches to history, but it is simply unfair to students if teachers leave out critical eras of history during students' thirteen-year journey through K–12 social studies. Because certain parts of the world get more attention than others in our history courses, curriculum mappers must stay alert to build the most seamless social studies program they can, given the difficult task of eliminating key periods because of time constraints. Common historical skills, such as analyzing primary source documents, sorting fact from fiction, and debating multiple sides of an issue, should also be clearly identified in maps. Range, or flexibility, makes sense in terms of providing students with opportunities to fully investigate areas of interest and issues that emerge naturally from the study of history.

• **Political Science.** Political science provides an opportunity for students to compare characteristics and features of various governments. The bias of parents and teachers on political issues is obvious to most children. What should be consistent in the United States is the opportunity to express our views in an active democracy (Glickman, 2003a). Although consistency on advocating a particular position is antithetical to good political science instruction, precise agreement is critical about what issues in the content will be examined.

• **Anthropology.** There can be a particularly interesting range of experiences in anthropology as children examine cultures. Artifact analysis, interviewing, and online exchanges with students around the world are now possible, given our advanced technologies. Clearly, anthropology selections are often some of the most sensitive in the school curriculum. Should the same cultures be examined at each grade level? Which ones should be left out? All anthropologists have worldviews shaped by their personal backgrounds. Thus, it becomes a more fluid and difficult field to achieve consensus in all areas, except for the identification of specific cultures. Learners can become modern anthropologists. The social sciences lend themselves to great excitement, argument, and investigation. They require careful analysis concerning consistency and flexibility.

Science

Science curriculum is based on a solid set of procedures found in the **scientific method**. This approach to inquiry is to be developed methodically and consistently over the school years. Many times confusion exists between introducing those methods and using them in a developmental fashion. In truth, I have seen maps beginning in 4th grade with entries indicating that the teacher is introducing the scientific method, plus other maps that continue to say that those skills are being introduced throughout high school. The map needs to show definite expansion and sophistication. High school students have already been introduced to the scientific method; they need to be challenged with more elaborate opportunities to use the method.

A key content issue in science is to agree on which **concepts** and bodies of information should be targeted—and at which grade levels. Sometimes the question of having a range of assessments proves problematic in the review process, although ultimately this question sparks a worthwhile debate. For example, one biology teacher in a middle school might use a multiple-choice test to ascertain student knowledge, whereas the neighboring biology teacher might use a class **lab**. Lab formats should be consistent year to year, even as the nature of the problems becomes more challenging. If we want to see "world class" science emerge, then we must encourage flexibility in science investigations by independent students, as in New York State's Science Research Program. Science departments that work with mapping tend to consider a set of more elaborate assessments to build consistent scientific competencies.

Performing and Fine Arts

Instruction in performing and fine arts reflects a dynamic range of approaches, creations, and student performances. By the same token, there is a striking consistency in the precise and incremental way that students move through the years in developing their personal expertise. Perhaps this consistency is because the outcomes of student work are public and visible. The performance nature of the arts points to the richness of variety in students' voices, yet also to the consistency of skill building that frequently occurs in our arts departments.

On the elementary level, the nature of art departments is such that one teacher might serve the entire population of K–5 learners over six years of elementary school. This arrangement provides an internal mechanism for monitoring the progress or regress of each learner. In high school, electives and graduation requirements dictate the possibilities for studio work, music performing groups, and choreography.

Physical Education

Physical education has always been a model for spiraling curriculum. Skills are clearly stated for the learner. The teaching goal is to improve individual student performance using the phrase "**personal best**," which points to the obvious range of students in any physical education class. Demonstrations of student work are constant, as are the standards for excellence. The role of the teacher is to enable learners to "revise" their performances without teacher interference. Physical education classes thrive on the interaction between individuals improving their skills and groups learning to work together. Unquestionably, there are gymnasiums where fierce competition and humiliation are forces to be reckoned with for students and for their teachers. Yet, in terms of the curriculum, the arts and athletics are often areas that wrestle effectively with the consistency and flexibility issues in the design of the curriculum map.

Teachers should develop the questions before reviewing the map that is building toward consensus. Those questions should reflect a sincere attempt to determine what is unique about each discipline. A school faculty can reflect on those features of each subject area that point to the need for consistency and those features that require attention to flexibility.

Interdisciplinary Curriculum

Interdisciplinary curriculum certainly emerges in the same spirit of review. The questions might be, "Which interdisciplinary units or courses should be requisite experiences for the students in our school? Which should be optional?" Perhaps an elementary teacher might wish to use an interdisciplinary **theme** to present an array of concepts from the targeted standards, whereas another teacher might deal with the standards discipline by discipline. Does it matter whether teachers address certain content topics differently? Does it matter to the learners whether certain standards are effectively taught through an approach that is straight disciplinary or interdisciplinary?

Answers to such questions are best found in the quality of student work. Assessing student progress and evidence of the skills provides insight into whether range or consistency is critical.

There is, however, one area of interdisciplinary concern that should definitely be consistent: the area of literacy. **Cross-disciplinary literacy** is requisite for students to perform in all classroom situations. Here, interdisciplinary review should be viewed in terms of consistent standards of writing, strategies for reading, opportunities for speaking, and a focus on targeted listening through active note-taking. A consistent focus on building (1) specific study skills, (2) interactive text reading strategies, and (3) editing and revising proficiencies should be a goal for a consensus map. A case cannot be made that erratic attention to language capacity-building is helpful to our learners. Mapping provides a remarkable opportunity to elevate literacy strategies in every classroom. In short, each math teacher is a writing teacher; each science teacher is a speech teacher; each art teacher is a reading teacher. We are all language teachers and enablers.

Conclusion

The focal point of this chapter has been to make a case for more intricate care in working toward curriculum consensus. Because the questions before educators are those dealing with making strong collective decisions, taking the time to examine each field and the sequences that make sense for learners is critical. The issue is not simply arriving at consensus. The premise developed here is that two variables—consistency and flexibility—are necessary. These two variables need to be examined according to the special characteristics of the curriculum for each discipline.

Long-Term Journey That Transformed a District

Ann Johnson and Jennie L. Johnson

How often has someone asked, "Why fix it if it isn't broken?" On the surface, the Ankeny Community School District in Ankeny, Iowa, didn't need fixing because it wasn't broken. Our local constituents, both town citizens and internal staff members, would not have considered transformation of our district as necessary 10 years ago. Yet, after starting our school improvement journey using curriculum mapping as a tool, we have, indeed, transformed. Our students have made marked improvement in performance, we have enhanced our leadership capacity on every level, and we have refined our focus and consistency in instruction. We have also used data to guide decisions in professional development and instruction, plus technology as a tool to systematize curriculum mapping.

The process of curriculum mapping became part of our system and focused our efforts in the following areas:

- Building leadership
- Moving from the individual maps to district maps
- Creating quality maps
- Connecting other district and state initiatives
- Providing research-based staff development
- Maintaining sustainability
- Creating a long-term vision

As with most trips, we have endured detours and encountered delays by forces we could not control. We have dealt with breakdowns and repairs in the process of school improvement and mapping. Despite it all, not only have we enjoyed the trip, but also—as so often happens on such a journey—we have learned more than we ever imagined.

The Ankeny Community School District

Ankeny is a suburban school district located just north of Des Moines, Iowa. It is a middle- to upper-level-income community in which students achieve well above the national average on norm-referenced tests.

Why did our district believe that we needed to rethink curriculum and assessment? The superintendent, the Superintendent's Advisory Committee (which consists of parents representing every program in the district), the Ankeny Taxpayers' Association, the Facilities Committee, and representatives from the teaching staff review had been studying the availability of student space in each building in the district and examining predictions for growth. Our district experiences phenomenal growth each year compared to other districts in the state. The student population usually grows from 150 to 225 students each year, and this growth has continued for at least eight years. The projections showed that growth would continue and probably increase over the years. To accommodate such growth, the district decided to redesign the structure of the buildings. At the beginning of the 1996–

1997 school year, the six elementary schools became kindergarten through 5th grade schools, the junior high schools became 6th and 7th grade middle schools, a newly constructed building became an 8th and 9th grade middle school, and the high school became a 10th through 12th grade school.

With this massive reorganization, two-thirds of the 350 teachers changed teaching assignments. In addition, an annual turnover of staff results from retirements and a growth of 45 to 55 new teachers each year. Therefore, the district had many teachers who were just starting their careers or were starting over with new curriculum. Many teachers who changed grade levels took their favorite units and activities with them, even though the topics of those units and activities were not in the district curriculum. Consistency was lacking in subjects taught by many different teachers. Gaps and repetitions surfaced in various curricula, depending on which teacher taught the course or subject. The taught curriculum, in many cases, did not resemble the district curriculum that was written into the courses of study. Many teachers were more concerned with covering more curriculum rather than the depth of knowledge and learning.

Need for Change

The associate superintendent for instruction determined through a curriculum audit that the district needed a common focus on curriculum. With the creation of new information at an ever-increasing rate, teachers, administrators, and parents questioned the validity of the seven-year curriculum cycle. Teacher volunteers and administrators were recruited to attend a school-restructuring conference in New York. Several of the Ankeny group attended a session by Dr. Heidi Hayes Jacobs on curriculum mapping. They were so excited that, upon their return, they proposed starting a pilot in mapping at the secondary buildings.

In the first year, we worked with 12 members of the secondary teaching and administrative staff who had attended the conference on curriculum mapping. This group became our leadership team for the curriculum mapping initiative. It held a professional development session for the teachers in the three buildings and asked them to map only their content. We soon learned that we needed to expand our leadership base in order to continue the effort in the entire district. The leadership group developed a plan for implementing the process using a time line and a plan for building leadership capacity. Now, eight years later, the district leadership looks quite different from what was in place when we began the process of curriculum mapping.

Leadership Transformation

The first step in the plan for building leadership capacity was to expand the group of teachers and administrators who had received training in the curriculum mapping process at the workshops conducted by Dr. Jacobs. The original group of teachers and administrators consisted of the secondary staff. Therefore, it was necessary to train elementary staff members and administrators. This new group of secondary and elementary teachers and administrators formed the original leadership team that was responsible for implementing the curriculum mapping process in all nine schools in the district.

At the end of the second year of implementation, the curriculum mapping leadership team distributed a survey to teachers and administrators. The survey was designed to determine the degree of implementation of the process in each school in the district. Upon analyzing the data collected from the survey, the team came to one undeniable conclusion: everyone was working hard at implementing the process, but it was obvious that not all schools had received the same message.

Therefore, step two of the leadership expansion plan was implemented. This step involved examining the leadership roles that existed in the district. At that time, the primary leadership roles in the district included the school administrators, the department chairs, and the grade-level leaders. Those roles had traditionally been management roles. The district needed leaders who could guide not only the curriculum mapping process but also the state-mandated Comprehensive School Improvement Process. After meetings with the Ankeny Teachers' Association, the associate superintendent of instructional services created a new leadership position: the building curriculum facilitator. Each elementary school has two building curriculum facilitators, and each secondary school has three. Teachers apply for these positions and are paid a yearly stipend. Over time, this job has come to encompass more than was originally intended, because those building curriculum facilitators and their principals have become the curriculum leaders and supporters in each school.

Role of the Building Curriculum Facilitators

At the beginning of each school year, the principal and the building curriculum facilitators meet with staff members and remind them of the building goals set by the entire staff for the new school year. The facilitators then review the curriculum goals for the year and distribute a time line and a list of products to be submitted to the principal and the curriculum office by the end of the year. In addition, they hand out an inservice schedule showing the professional development days reserved for mapping training and mapping work.

The facilitators also hold small group sessions, called "hold your hand help," for those people who want individual training and encouragement in the mapping process or who want assistance entering their maps

into the software that the district has chosen to house the maps and the data. The facilitators collect feedback and data from the staff in their buildings throughout the year, and they share that data at the monthly meeting of all facilitators, principals, and the curriculum team (consisting of the associate superintendent of instructional services; the district reading facilitator; and the two teachers on special assignment, who are curriculum and assessment specialists).

Those meetings are strategy sessions for coaching teachers in the curriculum mapping process and other state initiatives that the district has been able to integrate into the process. For example, after teachers had completed one map, the curriculum team noticed that the quality of the maps was not what it should be. The teachers had been shown how to align maps and to indicate the complexity of skills. Review of the maps, however, showed that most teachers needed more specific training.

In their search for an answer to this problem, the curriculum team developed a strategy that they call a quality cell, which is a sample unit covering a month's instruction. Those sample units are based on the mapping components described in Dr. Jacobs's book (1997a). Figures 4.1 and 4.2 show examples of two sample units: one for 1st grade math and another for 8th grade social studies students.

The curriculum team also developed a set of coaching questions, shown in Figure 4.3, to guide teachers' work as they review their maps for quality.

Fig. 4.1	**Curriculum Mapping (Sample Month or Unit)**

Subject/Course: _1st Grade Math_   **Month:** _____

Essential Questions
- How can patterns help me learn to add?
- What is adding?

Content
- Addition
  - Patterns
  - Associative principle
  - Counting and sets

Skills
- Explain a complex pattern.
- Distinguish between different kinds of patterns.
- Demonstrate the associative principle.
- Match one-to-one correspondence.
- Count to 20.
- Write numbers in sequential order to 20.
- Count sets of objects.
- Demonstrate an understanding of joining objects to make a larger group.

Assessments
- Use written addition exercise (write numbers to 20 and indicate the number of objects that would match); match one-to-one correspondence.
- Examine complex pattern (develop and label complex pattern with blocks).
- Review written computation of facts to 6.

Activities
- Use pattern blocks, and build certain types of patterns.
- Go on a pattern hunt, and look for different types of patterns.
- Use counting jars, and practice making sets.
- Use manipulatives to practice groups.

Source: Ankeny Community School District, Ankeny, Iowa.

Building curriculum facilitators and their principals were trained by a consultant on the use of the quality cell strategy at their next meeting. Each building in the district then used inservice time to train small groups of their staffs on the use of this strategy. The curriculum team made sure that one of its members was at every building meeting. The response was remarkable. Teachers were energized and ready to work on revising

Fig. 4.2	**Curriculum Mapping (Sample Month or Unit)**

Subject/Course: _8th Grade Social Studies: American Citizenship_   **Month:** _September_

Essential Questions
- Why have a Congress? How would your answer affect the citizens or people?
- Is there a better way?
- How does a bill become law?

Content
- Legislative Branch (core)
  - Powers of the Legislative Branch
  - Qualifications, duties, and powers of the members of the Legislative Branch
  - Organization of the Legislative Branch
  - Bill into law
    - Steps
    - Process
    - Effect(s) on citizens

Skills
- Describe the qualifications, duties, and powers of the members of the Legislative Branch (benchmark).
- Demonstrate the organization of the Legislative Branch.
- Identify the steps used in passing a bill into law.
- Demonstrate how a bill becomes law (benchmark).
- Analyze the effects of the Legislative Branch on citizens (critical skill).
- Develop opinions using supportive ideas (reading skill).

Assessments
- Examine graphic organizer about steps used to pass a bill into law.
- Know that bill-into-law performance task includes the following:
  - Roles are determined by qualifications, duties, and powers of the members.
  - Organization: House and Senate, committees, and process for bill into law.
- Determine if the persuasive paper "How is this law" is going to affect the students (the people).
- Debate (interdisciplinary project—social studies/language arts).
  - Why have a Congress?
  - Is there a better way?

Activities
- *Reading Strategy Activity: Knowledge Rating Scale*—vocabulary from Chapter 6
- Study guides for text reading
- Graphic organizer on qualifications, duties, and role of members and organization of the Legislative Branch
- Graphic organizer on steps used to pass bill into law
- "Who's Most Powerful" activity

Source: Ankeny Community School District, Ankeny, Iowa

their maps. At the semester break, each teacher turned in one cell of a map to the building curriculum facilitators for feedback. The teachers actually requested specific feedback to indicate whether they were on the right track before they revised the entire map. The building curriculum facilitators, along with their principals, have become the curriculum leaders in each building. Throughout all of the training and development of maps, the staff has relied on the curriculum leaders for training and expertise.

Role of the Building Improvement Team

Another group that provides leadership and support for the mapping process is the building improvement team, which consists of all building curriculum facilitators and principals, one combined committee representative from each building, and other teacher volunteers. The team performs the following:

• Planning and facilitating curriculum mapping and other curriculum work within each building

• Providing support so colleagues are successful at completing the curriculum goals

• Planning specific training

• Securing facilitators for the building staff to ensure successful completion of goals

• Providing feedback to the curriculum team to help address next steps in the curriculum mapping process

• Collecting and organizing maps and assessments

• Helping facilitate discussions about the use of data from maps, assessments, and surveys to inform instruction

The building improvement team is especially vital in linking the curriculum mapping process to school improvements. The team is responsible for ensuring that all initiatives in the district, of which curriculum mapping is one, are part of the school improvement process. Therefore, while the building improvement team works hand-in-hand with the building curriculum facilitators, its view is always on the bigger picture of school improvement.

Role of the Combined Committee

The combined committee provides the support structure for the massive project of systemizing curriculum mapping. This committee consists of teacher representatives from every school in the district in direct proportion to the number of students in each school building. Representatives from the elementary and secondary principals, the associate superintendent for instruction, the teachers on special assignment, a Board of Education representative, and a representative of the teachers' union executive board join those teacher representatives.

Fig. 4.3	**Coaching Questions for a Quality Month or Unit (Revised 9/14/2001)**

Essential Questions

• What overarching question(s) will serve to guide instruction and to push students to higher levels of thinking?

• What overarching questions might help students to link or connect a "Big Idea" or topic to other concepts or subjects?

• What specific questions might guide teaching and engage students in uncovering what is at the heart of each Big Idea or topic?

• What questions point beyond the unit to other transferable ideas or concepts?

• How are your essential questions, skills, and assessments connected or hooked?

Content

• What is the Big Idea or broad topic you will be covering?

• What are the major subcategories (chunks) on which you will spend a significant amount of time?

• What are the major underlying concepts for your Big Idea or broad topic?

Skills

• What are the enabling skills or processes that will ensure successful mastery of the Big Idea?

• What skills do students need to be successful at demonstrating the Big Idea, broad topic, or concept?

• On what skills do you spend a significant amount of time?

• Have you included the benchmarks and critical skills from your curriculum framework?

Assessments (culminating)

• What would you accept as evidence that students understand the Big Idea, broad topic, or concept?

• What product or performance will the students produce?

• Do the assessments allow students to demonstrate their learning or understanding in multiple ways?

Activities

• As you consider skills, what practice activities would you use to help students learn the concept?

Resources

• What specific support materials, books, field trips, videos, or Web sites do you use or incorporate in your teaching?

Source: Ankeny Community School District, Ankeny, Iowa.

The combined committee's primary responsibility is to supply monetary support to the schools to help them successfully complete their curriculum goals. The committee has agreed to combine all of the monies available to pay teachers to support curriculum mapping and school improvement efforts within the district. With the monetary resources aligned, the combined committee provides direction and leadership for the district improvement plan, plus additional professional development in areas or skills related to goals to help teachers and administrators successfully complete their goals.

Role of the Technology Team

To ensure that the curriculum mapping process results in data that can be used to meet goals and improve instruction, technology plays an important role. The district technology team works collaboratively with the curriculum team to provide vision for technology that will support curriculum mapping, instruction, and assessment. The technology team comprises the district technology coordinator, the teacher on special assignment for curriculum/assessment support, the associate superintendent for instruction, the executive director of finance, the superintendent, and the technology support personnel.

The work of this team includes the following:

• Planning and implementing the time line for training on the curriculum mapping software and other support software

• Training building curriculum facilitators and teacher leaders to assist in the software training sessions

• Working with software designers to troubleshoot problems to ensure successful implementation of the mapping software

The technology team has been instrumental in providing teachers with the skills they need to enter their maps and to collect data that will improve instruction.

Use of Data to Make Instructional Decisions

Implementing the curriculum mapping process and ensuring its place in the educational system requires leadership and support. The Ankeny Community School District has transformed its leadership structure as a result of the curriculum mapping process.

With the leadership in place to guide the curriculum mapping process, teachers completed drafts of their first maps under the direction of the building leadership teams. The drafts of maps were copied, and each school worked with its leadership teams and the curriculum office to prepare for the read-through process. This process is one of the most informative in the curriculum mapping process. Each school divided its staff into mixed groups. The mixed groups consisted of six to eight teachers from different grade levels and different subject areas within the school. Each person in the group was given copies of the maps of the other group members to review before the read-through session.

On the afternoon of the sessions, the groups met to review maps for four different pieces of information: "A-ha's," gaps, repetitions, and questions. Group members used the form shown in Figure 4.4 to record their observations of the maps.

The mixed-group members assigned the roles of facilitator, timekeeper, and recorder. Each person within the group was given two minutes to review the major components of a map. Then each member had two minutes to ask questions about that map. The questions were not to be critical of the map, but rather to elicit information about the curriculum from the person who wrote the map. (See Appendix 1 for information on how to organize the map read-through process.)

The building curriculum facilitators designed guided questions, shown in Figure 4.5, to assist teachers in eliciting information from the creator of the map.

The group's recorder captured the questions, answers, and areas that needed more discussion. On another professional development day, the process was repeated with groups that consisted of teachers who had taught in the same department or grade level. The recorders' sheets were compiled from the mixed groups, and the teachers addressed the data collected.

The review of the data was one of the most enlightening processes in curriculum mapping. The gaps and repetitions were easily identified, and those that could be resolved within the school were resolved during this review. Issues that needed to be addressed at the district level were compiled so the issues could be addressed at K–12 department meetings. The data collected from the maps provided the starting point for many curriculum initiatives. The K–12 department teams addressed the gaps and repetitions found during the read-through sessions, which resulted in changes in alignment of curriculum.

The review of the data from the individual maps revealed a lack of consistency in the maps of a subject or course that was taught by multiple teachers. For instance, more than 20 teachers taught 1st grade reading, but their curriculum maps were quite different. Those teachers agreed that the district needed a district map that contained the required content and skills each teacher should cover during the school year. They also felt that the required content and skills should not compose the entire curriculum. Teachers wanted time to personalize the content and skills taught in their classrooms. As a result of those discussions, the Ankeny Community School District created district maps, called curriculum frameworks, for every subject and course taught in the district. (See Appendixes 2 and 3.)

All of the information that teachers collected from the read-through of the curriculum maps whetted their thirst for more. They requested data from their maps that the district could not collect from the paper maps.

Fig. 4.4	Curriculum Mapping Read-Through Feedback

Facilitator: _____ **Date:** _____

A-ha's (What was something you learned?):	Possible repetitions noted:
Possible gaps noted:	Questions that need to be addressed about the maps:

Group of Participants: _____

Source: Ankeny Community School District, Ankeny, Iowa.

Technology—specifically, a software program that would house all of the maps in a database so that the information could be sorted—was the answer. After reviewing many different products, the district selected a program to meet all of our needs. With this program, teachers can print reports that tell them if they have covered all the content and skills listed in the district maps. They can also print a summary of the content standards and benchmarks covered in their maps.

Ways to Systematize the Maps

Armed with data from the maps plus assessment data that were aligned to the content and skills required in the district maps, the district looked for ways to systematize the use of data in making instructional decisions. The software technology made it possible to search all maps for specific topics. Because the state of Iowa requires the integration of reading, problem solving, technology, and skills from other subject areas into all subjects taught, the maps became the perfect vehicle for collecting data showing where those skills are taught.

For example, all elementary teachers teach reading as a defined subject. Therefore, they have a curriculum map for reading. However, in the secondary schools in Ankeny, reading is taught only in 6th and 7th grades. In grades 8–12, no reading class is required. Therefore, the district decided to train all secondary teachers to be teachers of reading in their own content areas. Then all teachers were required to integrate those reading skills

into their curriculum maps. The software made it possible to collect data on where those skills were being taught, so teachers could make decisions on the alignment of skills throughout the K–12 curriculum.

Using data from the maps and assessments has become a way of life for the teachers in the Ankeny Community School District. They have requested that the district work with the software company to develop a data module that could work with the curriculum mapping software. The teachers would like to have access to student data from the assessments that they have recorded on their curriculum maps and from the districtwide assessments administered by the district. Those assessments have all been aligned with district benchmarks and content standards, so the data would be aligned with the skills recorded in the curriculum maps. Having all the data and the information from the curriculum maps in a database program would allow teachers and administrators access to information aligned with the content and skills in the curriculum maps for entire classes or individual students. Such information provides teachers with facts they need to make instructional decisions that affect student learning.

Changes to the Paradigm for Professional Development

At the beginning of the curriculum mapping process, the teacher leaders and administrators

Fig. 4.5	Coaching Questions for Review
Data and Facts	"What use will you make of the information?" "How is the information related to . . .?"
Time	Sequence: "What happens first, second, . . .?" Duration: "How long . . .?" Rhythm: "How often . . .? How frequently . . .?"
Metacognition	"What were you thinking when . . .?"
Elaboration	"Tell me more about . . ."
Clarification	"Explain what you mean by . . ."
Intentionality	"For what purpose, toward what end . . ."
Prediction	"If you do . . ., what do you think will happen?"
Flexibility	"What if you were to . . .?" "How else might you . . .?"
Application	"What will you do with this?" "How will you apply this in another situation?"
Values/Beliefs	"What is important for you in . . .?" "What do you believe about . . .?"
Feelings	"What are your feelings about . . .?" "How do you feel about . . .?" "How do you feel when . . .?"
Commitment	"What are you choosing to do . . .?" "What follow-up needs to take place . . .?"

Source: Based on work by Art Costa and adapted from Costa and Garmston (1994).

realized that focused professional development was imperative to ensure successful implementation of the process. At that time, the professional development program in the district consisted of soliciting ideas from the nine school buildings and then developing programs for that particular year. The district provided two early dismissal days each month that afforded about an hour of professional development time after allowing for travel time so the teachers could go from their build-ings to the designated site. The district leadership team realized that implementing the curriculum mapping process in nine school buildings with 400 teachers would require extensive training in the process.

The first step in revamping professional development in the district consisted of examining the delivery system for professional development. The leadership team conducted extensive research in exemplary staff development and determined that the short, one-hour chunks of time did not allow enough time to present and discuss information or to have teachers work on developing maps and lessons. The unanimous decision was to request that the Board of Education change the two early dismissals per month to one half-day early dismissal per month for staff development. The board granted approval, and the leadership team began to develop a vision for three-year implementation of a staff development plan.

The building curriculum facilitators and the building administrators conducted surveys and compiled lists of professional development needs of teachers. When they compiled this information, the district leadership team quickly realized that one half-day per month would not be sufficient to accomplish all the training, support, and work time necessary for implementation. The building curriculum facilitators and the building administrators then scheduled a meeting with the combined committee. The larger group consisted of teachers, administrators, and board members. Its purpose was to determine the use of district funds for staff development and teacher projects. The combined committee examined other structures that were in place to see if those structures could also support professional development. The district was already offering classes on Saturdays for staff development or graduate credit. Those classes were revamped to provide additional training in curriculum mapping and other district initiatives and to provide teachers with time to

work on those initiatives in teams or departments. The combined committee also agreed to include the summer institute that was already in place in the professional development system. With one half-day per month, Saturday classes, and a four-day summer institute, the leadership team was able to develop a comprehensive professional development system.

As training in curriculum mapping and its implementation continued, the teachers asked for more time to work together on their maps, lesson plans, data analysis, integration of required skills into the maps and lesson plans, and assessment design in teams and departments. Again, the leadership team responded by adding work time to each professional development session and by creating structured and independent classes. Those classes support district initiatives by allowing each school to customize classes to the work being done in that school and district. Teachers have to meet specified criteria, provide evidence of the work they have done, and submit a summary of the outcome of their work. A portion of the hours worked can be on contract time, with the remainder of the hours coming outside the school day. The classes are also offered for staff development credit for license renewal.

In addition to the training opportunities, the curriculum mapping process furthered the evolution of the professional development plans designed by the school's curriculum facilitators and the principals in all schools. Each spring, the leadership teams in the buildings analyze the data collected from districtwide assessments and teacher surveys to determine the staff's development needs. A staff development map for the next school year is then created. That map lists the inservice days, study groups, and any other staff development opportunities offered by the school.

The curriculum team in the district revised the standard curriculum mapping form to fit the needs of the school's staff development plans (see Appendix 4). Those professional development maps contain the following components: essential questions, content, skills, evidence, time line/deadlines, and materials to bring. Each building staff member receives a staff development map at the fall teacher workshops. Those maps guide the professional development in each school and are based on the data collected during the previous school year.

All pieces of the staff development program had been focused on the implementation of curriculum mapping. Then, as curriculum mapping became part of the system, the focus shifted to the other state, federal, and district initiatives that are supported by the curriculum mapping process.

Effect of Curriculum Mapping

At the end of the school year, the district leadership team reflected on what curriculum mapping had done for the Ankeny Community School District in the areas of curriculum, instruction, and assessment. The team compiled this list of ways in which the process has enhanced the district's instructional programs:

• A focus for curriculum, instruction, and professional development

• Consistency in instruction and assessment

• Alignment of instruction to the content standards and benchmarks in all content areas, plus increased accountability for instruction

• Access to data about instruction, assessment, and student learning

• A vehicle for integration of skills, such as reading, into all subject areas

• An awareness of what other teachers in the department, team, or grade level are teaching

• An increased awareness of the researched-based link between teaching and learning

This focus on improving the district's instructional programs resulted in organizational and leadership changes, new ways of collecting and analyzing data, and a new paradigm for planning and implementing professional development. Curriculum mapping became the hub that focused the work of the district on enhancing student achievement. Every aspect of the work in the district emanated from that hub, and the hub served as an organizing force for bringing together the group of dedicated professionals who were charged with providing every child with a rich, coherent, and consistent instructional program across the grades. Curriculum mapping has allowed teachers and administrators to become dreamers and confident risk-takers in their quest to help all students become independent and lifelong learners.

Curriculum Mapping from an Independent School's Perspective

Stephen D. O'Neil

When I first read about curriculum mapping, I knew Minnehaha Academy in Minneapolis, Minnesota, was ripe for change. I looked at the academy through my lens as director of curriculum, a position I had been in for only a few months. In 1997, a five-year strategic plan was developed to guide Minnehaha Academy through 2002. On the basis of that plan, a Curriculum Development Task Force was formed in 1998 to examine how best to enhance the schoolwide integration of the preschool through 12th grade curriculum. The director of curriculum's position grew out of that work. The job description included a requirement "to provide leadership for the review, development, implementation, and coordination of curriculum preschool through 12th grade." In the summer of 1999, I accepted that position.

Faculty's Response to Curriculum Mapping

A year after I assumed the new position, we began to implement curriculum mapping. In the early stages, I asked the faculty to comment on the benefits of curriculum mapping. These are some of their responses:

- Curriculum mapping will be very helpful in planning and organizing schoolwide events.
- A lot of room exists for individuality.
- It is good to take a look at how I am teaching. This appraisal will influence how I teach in the future.

• Curriculum mapping is a good process for assessing the current curriculum materials being used.

• Once the map is completed, it will be very helpful for new faculty members, giving them a clear picture of what to teach.

• Curriculum mapping will be used in team meetings to see what everyone is doing in classrooms that month.

• It will encourage more collaboration within and across departments.

• It should eliminate unintentional overlapping of material.

• It should be a selling point for the school.

• I like seeing my colleagues' work; it helps me feel part of the big picture.

• Creation of the essential questions was of value to me because it forced me to consider what was an important priority about a certain unit I was teaching.

• I can see the value of curriculum mapping from a departmental perspective to survey what we are covering and where there might be gaps in our scope and sequence.

• I thought curriculum mapping gave me a big-picture view of what I do with my students.

Overview of Minnehaha Academy

Minnehaha Academy was founded in 1913 to provide a strong academic program rooted in the Christian faith. The school, located just a few miles from downtown Minneapolis, is divided into three divisions: upper school (grades 9–12), middle school (grades 6–8), and lower school (grades PreK–5). In addition to the campuses located in Minneapolis, a second lower school has been founded in suburban Bloomington, Minnesota.

Minnehaha Academy serves more than 1,200 students who represent more than 50 communities in the Twin Cities. The academy has more than 100 faculty members and offers a college preparatory program. The school is also recognized for its fine arts program and its emphasis on diversity, technology, and the integration of faith and learning.

Each school division has its own special curriculum emphasis. The lower school's core curriculum includes language arts, math, social studies, science, and Bible. Students attend classes in art, music, physical education, a world language, and computer instruction/library science. The middle school faculty teams provide a strong interdisciplinary curriculum that includes experiential education with field trips and interdisciplinary projects. Middle school students are required to take Latin in 6th grade, and in subsequent years to choose from Latin, German, Spanish, or French. The upper school offers a strong college preparatory curriculum. More than 100 courses, including 17 Advanced Placement/Honors courses, are offered each school year.

An education committee that represents faculty and administration at all levels of the school makes curriculum decisions. The education committee's mission is to provide a cross-campus platform for schoolwide communication focusing on educational trends, curriculum innovation and change, and faculty professional development. Some of its tasks include making recommendations regarding course and curriculum changes, plus monitoring the curriculum mapping process.

The education committee oversees a critical aspect of the curriculum review process by providing a forum to discuss curriculum change and effect. Before our adoption of curriculum mapping, the academy followed a five-year plan to review subject areas in grades 6–12. The lower school conducted a curriculum review using a different model. One or two disciplines were reviewed at the same stage in the cycle in a given year. According to the five-year plan, each subject area was assigned a different primary task to accomplish each year.

Curriculum Mapping Implementation: Early Seeds

In the fall of 1999, I read *Mapping the Big Picture: Integrating Curriculum and Assessment K–12* (Jacobs, 1997a). A few months later, I attended a curriculum mapping conference hosted by the Association for Supervision and Curriculum Development. I became convinced that the academy could benefit from curriculum mapping as a communication and review tool, so I presented the

concept to the education committee in the spring of 2000. A faculty member who served on the education committee wrote me the following letter in response to that presentation.

I think the curriculum mapping idea is wonderful, but I hope you're not planning much beyond selling the concept, presenting the examples, and giving faculty time to collect data in the fall. New and inexperienced faculty [members] may feel you are giving them an impossible task. Upper school faculty [members] might say they have no idea what they will actually cover under the new block schedule [that began in September 2000].

When I was department chair and I tried to construct charts for grammar, literature, writing skills, and so on, it was like pulling teeth even to get faculty to put anything on paper. That's where the principals come in.

Heidi [Hayes Jacobs] is absolutely correct that no one can know what each individual faculty member covers for sure; I like the concept of making each faculty member accountable for her curriculum. Will all three 9th grade English faculty members have to agree upon what goes in the 9th grade curriculum map, or will they start with three separate ones? Either way, it would be valuable.

I also like the "essential questions" versus "objectives" approach, especially the part about posting the questions on the wall.

But the most valuable part are phases 2–6 [curriculum review], once you get everything on paper. That is where other people will see what I have seen in Learning Lab [for students needing additional academic support] for years: the gaps and repetitions she speaks of. I had a librarian mention that "everybody" does pilgrims in November. I wonder which parts of American history our students have had so many times [that] it actually creates boredom in future years.

And the spiraling assessments—some faculty [members] will salivate at that concept.

I think your best tactic for selling this to the faculty is that of getting their curriculum together in a computer format that will be easily updated in the future. Emphasize that it is a "fluid" process, and assure them that this isn't about evaluation of their teaching or trying to force everyone into a curricular mold. At the start, it is all about getting information that only they have.

Let's keep talking. I am behind you 100 percent on this one.

At the beginning of the summer of 2000, I led a retreat for the academy's president and the principals of the three schools so I could build a case for curriculum mapping and for getting their support to implement the initiative. We discussed ideal conditions with our curriculum organization flow chart, curriculum review cycles, course proposals, and specific curriculum focus areas. We agreed on the following guiding principles to steer our school's curriculum:

• Clear communication about curriculum occurs between the three schools (lower, middle, and upper).

• The curriculum is coordinated between the two lower school campuses.

• Faculty members within the same school communicate with each other about their curriculum.

• The curriculum review cycle addresses gaps, overlaps, or inconsistencies in the PreK–12 curriculum.

• The curriculum review cycle operates in PreK–12 with each subject area.

• The curriculum review cycle encourages different subject areas to collaborate and have an interdisciplinary focus.

• Long-range planning fosters a thoughtful and proactive process that leads to a cutting-edge curriculum.

• Systems are in place to assess and evaluate curricular changes during the curriculum review cycle.

• The curriculum review cycle helps determine which courses should be added or deleted from the curriculum at the 6–12 levels.

• The school's curriculum is enhanced through the use of technology, and its scope and sequence across PreK–12 are monitored as technology changes.

• The school's curriculum reflects racial, ethnic, and economic diversity in different subject areas, and coordination of diversity with the curriculum exists.

• The school's curriculum addresses accreditation target goals that have been established by each school division.

• The curriculum allows for a balance between faculty independence in curricular decisions and a curriculum that best serves our students.

• Time is provided for faculty members to work on curriculum development and to collaborate on curriculum.

The president and the principals agreed that change needed to occur, and they gave their support to this new undertaking. That summer, I began to work with a member from our school's technology team to develop a curriculum mapping, Web-accessible database. He used FileMaker® Pro, a database software application that is managed from our Web site. In approximately 80 hours, he created an internal database that was simple to use and that met our needs. In the early months of the 2000 school year, the director of technology formed a database focus group to evaluate the curriculum mapping database, provide input on how comprehensive the database should be, and recommend professional development necessary to use the tool.

Our database is very easy to use and offers a variety of word search options to analyze the curriculum. Faculty members have a calendar-based map (months on one axis and essential questions, content, skills, and assessments on the other axis) for each subject or course they teach. Figure 5.1 provides an example of a September curriculum map for a history course.

The database has the capability to organize all curriculum maps by department, division, or grade level (PreK–12). Key word searches can locate words in the following ways:

• Wherever the word exists in all maps

• Wherever the word exists in essential questions, content, skills, or assessments

• Wherever the word exists in maps by department, division, or grade level

The search page for our database, as seen in Figure 5.2, also allows for the opportunity to integrate key school initiatives (i.e., technology) into the search capability.

We can search for the word "renaissance," as seen in Figure 5.3, and not only find it in a variety of departments (fine arts, social studies, and English), division levels, and grade levels, but also find the months in which the topic is taught.

To say the least, the database search function has allowed faculty curriculum reviewers to more carefully analyze the scope and sequence of each subject and to determine interdisciplinary opportunities at the same grade level. The overall database has freed our faculty to more easily navigate the intricacies of curricular change and renewal.

Fig. 5.1   Sample Curriculum Map for European History

Faculty Home Page	Mapping Home Page	Search Classes	Search Maps	Guidelines	Glossary	Report a Bug

You are not logged in—you may not edit this map.

Stephen O'Neil's AP European History

Upper	Social Studies	Grade(s) 12

Show Full Year Map   **Other Classes Taught by Stephen O'Neil**

September

Essential Questions:	Why did the Italian Renaissance not begin in England? Why did the Italian Renaissance occur during the 14th and 15th centuries? Is Machiavelli's political leader moral, immoral, or amoral? How did various works by Renaissance writer's shape the age? Was the Reformation primarily an economic event? How have various modern Protestant denominations been influenced by 16th century reformers.
Content:	Origins of the Italian Renaissance Italian and Northern European Art—"Sister Wendy" video Machiavelli's *The Prince* Italian and Northern European writers and philosophers Protestant Reformation in Northern Europe Martin Luther: theological positions (sola fida, communion, separation of church and state, priesthood of all believers, sola scriptura) Anabaptists: separation of church and state, baptism, communion, scripture John Calvin: theocracy predestination English Reformation: Henry VIII, dissolution of monasteries, Church of England
Skills:	Analyze the differences and similarities between Italian and Northern European Renaissance art Evaluate causes for Protestant Reformation using PERSIA model Debate Luther's position with van Eyck's position (Roman Catholic) Analyze six primary documents written by Martin Luther Define the theological differences between the 16th century church reformers
Assessment:	Reports on Italian and Northern European Renaissance writers and philosophers (brief biography, description and analysis of best-known work, and an evaluation of the Renaissance ideals they displayed) Read a few chapters from Hachiavelli's *The Prince* and prepare a summary of its contents with an analysis of moral, immoral, or amoral behavior Review questions from chapter PERSIA model grid to place value on various causes of Protestant Reformation

This class's maps were last updated 6/16/2003

Source: Database software developed by the Technology Department at Minnehaha Academy, Minneapolis, Minnesota.

Fig. 5.2   Sample Curriculum Map Search Database

| Faculty Home Page | Mapping Home Page | Search Classes | Search Maps | Guidelines | Glossary | Report a Bug |

Search for curriculum maps that contain the following words:
(Enter more information to narrow the search, or less to broaden it.)

Anywhere in the Map:

Or Only in the Specified Field(s):

Essential Questions:

Content:

Skills:

Assessment:

You may also limit your search to only those classes that also match the following criteria:

Teacher:

Department: (any department)

School: (any school)

Grade: (any grade)

Search Curriculum Maps

Key Topics

Technology Integration

- word processing
- spreadsheet
- PowerPoint

Multicultural Focus

- stereotype
- slavery
- ethnocentrism

Writing Types

- Type 1
- Type 2
- Type 3
- Type 4

Student Assessments

- models
- reports
- blueprints
- anthology

Source: Database software developed by the Technology Department at Minnehaha Academy, Minneapolis, Minnesota.

Map of Our Reality: Phase I

During the 2000–2001 school year, the faculty spent three professional development days (spread from August through January) learning about curriculum mapping and how to use the new database. On the first professional development day in August, I introduced curriculum mapping to the entire faculty. I intentionally emphasized that this approach was not an easy endeavor, and I moved the focus from a discussion about faculty concerns to a discussion about providing the best curriculum for our students.

On the other two professional development days, the focus group representatives provided technology training for the faculty. Each faculty member spent time mapping some area of the curriculum. The faculty was grouped by subject area in different technology labs around campus. It was exciting to listen to the curriculum conversations taking place as faculty members worked next to each other, mapping their curriculum for the first time and, in some cases, sharing their curriculum with another department member for the first time. As the work progressed, administrators and teachers had many questions. Those questions and the answers we provided can be found in Appendix 5.

By June 2001, faculty members had mapped their entire curriculum in all subject areas for the calendar year. The Web-accessible database for curriculum mapping had worked almost flawlessly. The faculty was impressed with the ease of use and with the quality of the curriculum-mapping database. They could work on it from home, could edit and make changes easily, and could publish their curriculum on the school Web site.

Action Plan

In July 2001, I became principal of the upper school, and a new director of curriculum was hired. Under new leadership, we are now moving forward with the review phases. We anticipate that we will need a total of two years to move through the additional phases of curriculum mapping that will serve as our review cycle.

In the second year of curriculum mapping, each faculty member edited the maps of other teachers who taught in the same grade level, building, or department. During the editing process, each teacher worked alone and used a standardized system—such as colors and symbols or a rubric template—to note new information, repetition, gaps, new assessment opportunities, and potential areas for integration. After completing the initial editing, individual faculty editors met in about 15 groups organized by divisions or departments, depending on the subject matter. Each group member shared his or her individual findings. Those findings were then recorded. This was a time to share observations, not to decide on changes. All faculty members attended a large group

Fig. 5.3   Sample Curriculum Map Search Results

Faculty Home Page	Mapping Home Page	Search Classes	Search Maps	Guidelines	Glossary	Report a Bug

School	Department	Teacher	Class	Grades	Last Updated	Months
Upper	Arts	Nate Stromberg	Art 2B	10, 11, 12	6/12/2001	Jan.
Middle	Arts	Ronie George	Art 7	7	6/14/2001	Jan.
Upper	Social Studies	Timothy Whalen	Early American History	11, 12	6/13/2001	Feb.
Upper	English/Language Arts	David Lindmark	English 11	11	1/13/2003	Mar.
Upper	Social Studies	Timothy Whalen	European History	11, 12	6/8/2001	Sep., Jan.
Upper	Arts	Michael Olsen	Men's Choir	9, 10, 11, 12	10/17/2002	Jan., Feb.
Upper	Arts	Enanna Massey	Orchestra	9, 10, 11, 12	11/4/2002	Nov.
Upper	Social Studies	David Glenn	Recent American History	11, 12	6/12/2001	Mar.
Upper	Social Studies	Timothy Whalen	Recent American History	11, 12	6/8/2001	Feb.
Middle	Social Studies	Wally Borner	Social Studies 7	7	11/4/2002	Mar.
Upper	Arts	Michael Olsen	Women's Chorale	9, 10, 11, 12	10/17/2002	Jan., Feb.
Upper	Social Studies	David Glenn	World History	9	11/14/2001	Dec., May
Lower–South	Arts	Karen Wald	Music	1	5/23/2003	May
Upper	Social Studies	Elizabeth VanPilsum	Modern European History	12	10/29/2002	Sep., Feb.
Upper	Social Studies	Stephen O'Neil	AP European History	12	6/16/2003	Sep., Oct., Nov.
Middle	Social Studies	Brian Cripe	Social Studies	6	1/16/2003	Feb.

Source: Database software developed by the Technology Department at Minnehaha Academy, Minneapolis, Minnesota.

review, at which time recorders from each of the small groups reported their findings. Those findings were recorded and distributed so that the entire faculty could comment on emerging patterns.

In the third year, we will finally have the opportunity for minor and major editing. Meeting in departments, teams, and divisions, the faculty will identify areas that can be easily changed on the basis of the report from the large group review. Some changes can be easily made without involving the education committee. Other changes will be brought to the education committee for review. Changes that are based on the recommendation of that committee will occur through the department. For significant changes, task forces will be set up to examine the change and to conduct additional research. The task forces will report their findings back to the education committee, which again will recommend changes.

Curriculum Mapping's Effect

It is exciting to see the initial and sustained effect that curriculum mapping has had. Faculty members have become more responsible for their curriculum, knowing that other faculty members can view their curriculum. They have developed pride in their curriculum now that it has become more public; because it is more public, many teachers have set their standards even higher.

The faculty appreciates the autonomy that curriculum mapping allows them. Dr.

Jacobs refers to it as "informed autonomy." At an independent school such as Minnehaha Academy, faculty members appreciate that they have individual autonomy with curriculum decisions. Curriculum mapping allows for this but fosters communication to decide if such autonomy best serves students. The communication between faculty members in the same school and increased levels of communication among faculty members at the same grade level or in the same department has improved significantly.

Newly hired teachers are thrilled to have maps from the faculty members they replaced. Often, one of the first questions asked at an interview or after a candidate accepts a teaching position is "Will you describe the curriculum for this course or class?" It is wonderful to respond to those candidates that curriculum maps are available.

Faculty members are able to renew their curriculum when they sit down to write out their first draft with curriculum mapping. Often, the essential questions that we use with curriculum mapping will help faculty members set priorities for what is important. Teachers take time to assess the big picture. Because curriculum mapping is not top down but rather from the grass roots, I have noticed a positive energy that is created as faculty members renew their living curriculum.

Some teachers have begun to talk more about a common vocabulary of words to discuss the same curricular item. There is also new discussion about scaffolding of complex vocabulary and ideas throughout the curriculum.

As the director of curriculum for Minnehaha Academy from 1999 to 2001, I was excited to observe curriculum change from a birds-eye view. Curriculum conversations in the faculty lounge occur more since we implemented curriculum mapping. The faculty members are very aware that Minnehaha Academy's curriculum has had redundancies and gaps. They now see a big picture of a student's career at academy as that student moves from preschool through 12th grade. They see the curricular implications of each student's experience in all of his or her classes each week. They can see how their individual curriculum fits into the school's overall curriculum.

Curriculum mapping has provided institutional focus as we address issues related to our accreditation target goals. It has also offered greater efficiency as a tool to take multiple initiatives, such as technology integration and diversity, and to wrap them into our work with curriculum mapping. Those initiatives now work in greater concert with our curriculum efforts.

Finally, a new course application form, shown in Figure 5.4, was adopted during our work with curriculum mapping for teachers in grades 6–12. It was intentionally aligned with our mapping efforts.

There have been noticeable areas of effect on our students. As teachers mapped their curriculum, they fine-tuned their work with students. Now, some faculty use essential questions—instead of using student objective statements—as a focal tool to organize learning and student inquiry. Essential questions are sets of questions used to frame curriculum work around artificial concepts (Jacobs, 1997a). Some faculty members use such questions on course syllabi along with introductions to units or concepts.

Students are the most important impact group. However, because we have not concluded the full review, the greatest effect at Minnehaha Academy is yet to come. For the sake of each student, it is critical to take the curriculum mapping initiative forward the entire way. Ultimately, students will reap substantial benefits from our curriculum mapping efforts. Their gain will be our most fulfilling reward.

Fig. 5.4	**Course Change Application for Minnehaha Academy, Grades 6–12 Curriculum**

Directions: Respond to the following in a typed format.

Application date:

Department:

Type of course change (add, remove, status change [required/elective or grade level]):

Course title:

Credits and time frame:

- Will the course be a trimester (middle school), semester, or full-year course?
- Which trimester(s) or semester(s) will the course offering occur?
- If a full-year course, will the course be offered every year?

Required or elective:

Grade level:

Prerequisite(s):

Course description:

In the description answer the following:

- What objectives or essential questions will guide the course?
- What content will be covered?
- What skills will students learn?
- What assessment tools will be used to measure student progress?

Data supporting need for change (e.g., curriculum mapping, student needs, research, assessment tools [parent/student surveys, SAT/ACT], changing college preparatory expectations):

Rationale for course change:

How might this course change affect any of the following issues?
- Integrating the Christian faith into the curriculum
- Fostering greater diversity in the curriculum
- Providing greater academic diversity within a department or at Minnehaha Academy
- Promoting an interdisciplinary curriculum
- Integrating technology into the curriculum

How would a course change affect other courses within the department or in other departments?

Budget implications:

Proposed date for change to occur:

Source: Minnehaha Academy, Minneapolis, Minnesota.

6 Principal's Role in the Curriculum Mapping Process

Mary Ann Holt

For the past 12 years, I have been involved with curriculum mapping—first as a building principal at the Chattanooga School for the Liberal Arts (CSLA) and then as a consultant guiding other schools and school systems through the mapping process. Through those experiences, I have learned many practical lessons about using curriculum mapping as a powerful tool. The focus of this chapter is to share with you what I learned about mapping from my positions as a CSLA principal and as a consultant. From my perspective, mapping is the most powerful process I have found to raise student achievement and teacher esteem. The state of Ohio recently recognized curriculum alignment through mapping as the most frequently cited strategy used to raise student achievement (Ohio Statewide Administrators Conference, 2001). It is my goal to share with you the lessons I have learned about mapping.

Principals encounter many struggles in their work in elementary, middle, or high schools. Each building is unique in configuration, numbers of teachers and students, student demographics, programs, and other characteristics. As you begin to consider mapping as an initiative, I am sure that you have many questions, such as these:

- Do I have the support to carry out this initiative?
- How can I convince my staff that this is not a passing educational fad?
- Where will we find the time to implement mapping?
- With all my other duties, how can I support and help lead this process?

Mapping made me rethink my role as a principal. The old army model of "top down" just does not work in the 21st century. Principals must build a community of learners, and it is the principal's role to develop and nurture that community. Curriculum mapping provides the channels of communication about how the work of schools should be done. The focus must always be on what the child needs in order to be a successful learner and, hence, a citizen of the world. Communication must be open and honest. As a principal, you need to be willing to assure your staff that mapping will not be used against them. The goal of mapping is to have a spiraling and challenging curriculum that is developed by the teachers and will meet and exceed the level of standards your system or state requires.

As teachers map their classroom curriculum, they may find gaps and redundancies, which means they must be willing to change what they teach if what they are currently teaching does not benefit the child. Certainly, this is challenging, but the rewards are worth the time. Teachers learn and share what they do, and they become more willing to work across the grade levels as well as within their grade or subject area. As their principal, you will be more than a cheerleader. You will be the one to whom they look for guidance.

Given the importance of communication and collegial support necessary for mapping to succeed, it is my advice that you not attempt this undertaking alone. Form a support group within your staff, and allow the members of the group to attend training and to do the research with you. I refer to this group as a planning/training team.

My goal is to act as your coach in areas where questions always arise and to provide suggestions and ideas based on my experience both as a principal and as a consultant. This chapter is divided into the following critical components and key decisions in the process:

• Training a school-based team
• Planning for implementation
• Finding time for mapping
• Presenting mapping to the staff
• Selecting a format and entering data
• Processing and using data, plus aligning the standards
• Sustaining the process: forming and using site-based councils

Training a School-Based Team

As the leader of your school, you must make sure you and your staff are trained on the entire process of mapping. Take time with a team of teacher leaders to plan for implementing the process in your school. Before the team attends training sessions, it is helpful for each member to read *Mapping the Big Picture: Integrating Curriculum and Assessment K–12* (Jacobs, 1997a). This short, readable book clearly lays out the steps in the mapping process. After team members have read the book, you should have a candid discussion about what mapping might do for your school.

At this point, you and your team are ready to schedule training sessions, which are available through various professional organizations or individual consultants (see Curriculum Mapping Resources, pp. 170–71). Another good resource is a video series titled *Curriculum Mapping: Charting the Course for Curriculum Content* (ASCD, 1999). The video series, filmed at the K–8 Chattanooga School for the Liberal Arts and at New Paltz High School in New Paltz, New York, shows discussions among teachers, principals, school board members, and Dr. Heidi Hayes Jacobs about various aspects of the mapping process. Dr. Jacobs's Web site (http://www.curriculumdesigners.com) is another good resource.

The principal's leadership and involvement in the training sessions are critical, because when teachers know that the principal is committed, they are much more likely to support the initiative. When the leadership team's training is complete, the next step is to plan for implementation. The recommended time to plan is a year, although many schools have been able to plan in less time.

Planning for Implementation

Planning for implementation requires serious deliberation about both long- and short-term issues. Mapping is a long-term process, not a final product, and it takes several years to fully implement. Therefore, it is important to make careful and thoughtful plans that won't overwhelm both teachers and the principal. Analyze the climate of your school by addressing the following questions: How do teachers approach new initiatives; and who are the trailblazers, the pioneers, the settlers, and the stay-at-homes?

Philip Schlecty (1993), CEO of the Center for Leadership in School Reform, wrote an article titled "On the Frontier of School Reform with Trailblazers, Pioneers, and Settlers," which discusses the roles that people play in the change process. It is a good article for your planning team to discuss as you decide how to support the various factions that are part of your faculty. Because mapping changes the way you work in the curriculum area, many teachers will be apprehensive. They are tired of the "pendulum swing" or, as they refer to it, the "flavor of the year." Therefore, it is critical that teachers understand mapping as an ongoing process that, if done correctly, produces great gains in both teacher and student achievement.

Jane Rankin and her team of teachers in the College Station Independent School District in College Station, Texas, addressed the planning issues by developing a time line, which is adapted as Figure 6.1.

Short-term planning involves determining what can be accomplished within the first year. In an elementary school, training and mapping one area of the curriculum is a reasonable goal for the first year. In middle and high schools, mapping two or three classes may be sufficient. The process of

Fig. 6.1	College Station Independent School District Time Line for Curriculum Mapping: Year 1, 2001–2002	
Month	**Action Steps**	**Who's Responsible**
September	• Have initial curriculum coach (CC) meeting.	• Deputy Superintendent for Curriculum and Instruction • Director of Curriculum
September	• Identify a mapping cadre at each campus.	• Campus CC
September	• Meet with CCs to brainstorm how to introduce curriculum mapping to campus mapping cadres.	• Director of Curriculum
October	• Make November 1 the target date for a template.	• Lead Technology Facilitator • Director of Curriculum
October	• Introduce curriculum mapping to mapping cadres. CCs should have completed maps.	• Campus CC
October–November	• Mapping cadres create curriculum maps (due December 1).	• Campus CC • Mapping Cadres
December	• Debrief with mapping cadres regarding curriculum mapping process. • Have CCs plan January 3 as district staff development day.	• CCs • Director of Curriculum
January	• Have district-wide staff development day. Introduce curriculum mapping to district staff (a.m.). • Have teachers create diary curriculum maps for August–December (p.m.).	• CCs • Director of Curriculum • Teachers
January–February	• Create projected map for spring semester (January–May).	• Teachers
February–March	• Conduct individual read-throughs.	• CCs • Teachers
April	• Use small- and mixed-group reviews.	• CCs • Teachers
May	• Conduct individual read-throughs of elective maps. • Plan large-group review (faculty meetings).	• CCs • Teachers

Source: Jane Rankin, College Station Independent School District, College Station, Texas.

entering the data usually takes about three to five months.

If "real time" data are entered for the first five months of the school year and projected data are entered for the remainder of the year, there will be time before the end of the year for the maps to be analyzed. This process helps teachers see how maps are developed and how they are going to be used.

Another short-term planning activity is to develop a clear definition of mapping to present to the staff. Just as journalists are trained to answer certain questions, teachers will likely want answers to the following:

- *What* is the mapping all about?
- *Who* will guide teachers through the process?
- *When* will they find time to do the mapping?
- *Where* are data on the effectiveness of mapping?
- *How* will mapping benefit my students and me?

You and your team must be prepared to answer these reasonable questions. As you work through the process, you will find the answers.

As you plan, remember that flexibility is the key to successful projects. Therefore, be willing to listen, act, revise, and share your vision with all participants. Map your plans for staff development. Give careful attention to the format teachers will use to enter data. Pencil and paper entries are time-consuming. A computer program is much more efficient.

Therefore, give planning time for determining how to meet technology needs.

Finding Time for Mapping

The use of teacher time is the number one issue and must be addressed up front. Use a spreadsheet, such as the one shown in Figure 6.2, to chart how teacher time in your school and the district is currently being used.

Decide what activities might be taken off teacher's plates to free up time. For example, look at the initiatives teachers are currently involved in, and decide which ones can be put on hold to allow time for mapping. A word of caution—many times principals are guilty of piling on new ways of doing things every year. We are always looking for the "best practice." The problem with this approach is that we need to know where these new practices fit within the curriculum. It is hard to determine the fit when you are not sure exactly what the actual curriculum is. Therefore, putting new initiatives on hold until you have mapped a curriculum is a good thing to do.

Because entering data in one curriculum area in the elementary school takes about three to five months, it is a good idea to begin by mapping an area, such as social studies, that does not have as many standards. Middle and high school teachers can possibly map three preparations in the same time frame. The time difference is because elementary teachers have more fundamental

Fig. 6.2	How Is Teacher Time Being Used?										
Grade Level	Science	Math	Social Studies	Language Arts	The Arts	Physical Education	Career/ Technology Education	Special Education	Guidance	Media/ Technology
K										
1										
2										
3										
4										
5										
6										
7										
8										
9										
10										
11										
12										

Source: Mary Ann Holt.

skills to teach and, therefore, their maps require more time to develop.

The following suggestions on how to find time for mapping may be useful as you begin the process:

• *Use staff meetings as time for mapping.* Develop a weekly or daily newsletter to share as much school business as possible so you can allow time in faculty and staff meetings to work on mapping.

• *Use rotating groups of substitute teachers.* Many systems release teachers for a half-day at a time and request that they have their mapping materials ready and that they find a quiet, interruption-free workplace. Determine how much is accomplished in those half-day sessions, and plan for more days if necessary. Teachers appreciate the half-day schedule because they are not absent from their classes for a full day.

Seeking grant money to finance planning time is another way to support the mapping process. Many organizations and foundations may be interested in supporting work in which curriculum mapping is to be a key tool for solving a specific problem. You don't know unless you ask. Ask your support team and your teachers for other ideas. Teachers are creative; if they see the benefits of mapping, they will come up with viable ideas—for example, funding mapping as a tool to address a literacy problem. As you address

the issue of time, remember that teachers appreciate being validated for the time they are currently spending in and out of school on preparation, training, and other tasks.

Cindy Gaston, a former CSLA teacher, made these comments about the time spent in the mapping process:

> When I first began the process of curriculum mapping, I was skeptical. I thought of it as one more thing to do that wouldn't affect my day-to-day teaching. However, I underestimated its usefulness to me as an individual teacher. Mapping has empowered me as a professional to develop a coherent curriculum for my students. I am able to design a curriculum that teaches what is really important and integrates content in a way that makes sense for kids. I can also use the maps as an essential communication tool with parents and other teachers. It was worth every minute I put into it.

Another comment that reaffirms the importance of finding the time for mapping is by Roger Taylor during a 1998 National School Conference Institute workshop: "If you don't have time to do it right, when will you have time to do it over?" Mapping saves not only time, but also money. It enables principals and teachers to focus on the needs for instruction and to avoid the many redundancies that occur.

Presenting Mapping to the Staff

Because many staff development sessions are perceived as boring and mundane, plan to involve the staff in a stimulating warm-up activity. The following activity, which is from a school in which I worked, really set the stage for presenting mapping to the staff:

The Treasure Hunt Activity

Three boxes of "treasures" are hidden on the school grounds. Teachers are divided into three teams. Each team is given a map that might lead the teachers to the treasures. One team's map contains redundant directions that take the teachers back to the same places, while the second team's map has huge gaps of information that are thoroughly confusing and frustrating. The third team's map is well documented and leads that team quickly to the treasures. After the activity, the faculty members discuss what they did and how it relates to what is going on with the curriculum and their students.

The activity set up the idea of the usefulness of maps in communicating the curriculum between and among teachers.

Another school, Spring Creek Middle School in Spring Creek, Nevada, began the mapping process by developing a satisfaction survey. The goal of the survey, shown in Figure 6.3, was to foster a discussion on mapping.

Warm-up activities build the background and motivate teachers' need for learning about the mapping process. Members of the planning team may conduct training sessions, or you can contract with a consultant. Be prepared to answer the many questions that arise, and be willing to look for answers as training proceeds. The trainers must create an attitude of trust because many teachers fear the maps will be used against them. The principal must assure teachers that the maps are essential to enhance student performance and to determine the school's real curriculum.

Honesty is an issue and must be addressed at the beginning of the mapping process. One teacher shared with me that she wasn't worried about showing me her map, but she was worried about what her peers might think about what she had, or had not, taught. This issue can be handled by having the teachers discuss what the difference is between an "ideal map" and a "real map" and which of the two is the most useful to the child. Affirm to your teachers that the school staff is striving for the ideal and is communicating with each other through the maps to reach their goal of helping each other help the children become more successful learners. Encouraging this type of attitude sets up a powerful, positive climate. Teachers become less defensive, more sharing, and more willing to become a learning and teaching community.

Modeling and illustrating the different phases of mapping are excellent training

Fig. 6.3	**Teacher Survey Activity**

Directions: How will we present curriculum mapping to our faculty?

If your answer below is YES to the question, give yourself 5 points; if NO, give yourself 1 point.

1. Are you a conscientious teacher who never has enough time to get it all done?

    Yes ____   No ____

2. Do you ever ask your students, "Didn't you learn how to do that in 4th grade? I think it was taught then."

    Yes ____   No ____

3. Do you spend your own money on lessons that have already been taught?

    Yes ____   No ____

4. Are you frustrated because you found out that Egyptology, cells, biomes, and so forth, were already taught to your students?

    Yes ____   No ____

5. Are you wondering what is going to happen to all the work we did on curriculum last year?

    Yes ____   No ____

6. Are you sure you've embedded the local and state curriculum objectives and standards into your teaching plans?

    Yes ____   No ____

7. Do you want an answer that will make your job the career you've always wanted it to be?

    Yes ____   No ____

8. Is what our students are learning essential to their success in future grades?

    Yes ____   No ____

9. Is accountability for both teachers and the school going away?

    Yes ____ (1 point)   No ____ (5 points)

10. Has your core team been successful in following through with your interdisciplinary units?

    Yes ____   No ____

If you scored more than 35 points, you need curriculum mapping!

Source: Antoinette Cavanaugh, Spring Creek Middle School, Spring Creek, Nevada.

strategies. Use visuals or a computer presentation to keep teachers centered on the process. Share time lines developed by the support team, and ask teachers to participate in refining the time line. (See Appendix 6 for a checklist to guide your initial phases of mapping.) Present some solid examples of what an effective map looks like. Ask members of your support team to map their curriculum areas and to share those maps with the teachers.

It is critical to keep teachers focused and on task during this beginning phase. Maryville High School developed "10 Steps to Curriculum Mapping" and "A Few Do's and Don'ts of Curriculum Mapping" (see Figures 6.4 and 6.5). At critical times, the staff and administrators on the Maryville planning team put these items in teachers' mailboxes. Developing checklists for your teachers as you work through the phases of the implementation process helps you avoid the "implementation dip."

Selecting a Format and Entering Data

Selecting a format for gathering data is essential and should be decided on quickly. The use of computer technology expedites the entire process. Paper and pencil entry of data is time consuming and has limited use. Because maps need to be upgraded on a regular basis, computers can easily accomplish the task and can be used to house the data.

Some issues to address include what level of expertise the staff has in using technology and whether training is needed to help teachers feel comfortable entering their mapping data on computers.

You can either purchase a software program or develop your own. If you elect to purchase software, preview it before you make the purchase. Schools and systems that have developed their own software either develop it to be used on the Internet or to be networked within their schools. Take time before deciding which is best for your school.

The next step in this phase is to illustrate to the staff how to enter the data on the system that has been either chosen or developed. It is critical that teachers enter their own individual data. Many teachers may tell you that they plan together, and, therefore, they teach the same things. However, one teacher might ask students to list the steps in the cycle of a mealworm, while another might ask students to list, describe, and illustrate the steps. Both teachers are teaching about the cycle of the mealworm, but the latter class is required not only to list the steps, but also to describe and illustrate the life cycle. Therefore, the instructional outcomes are different. Precise skill entries make the data more accurate and, therefore, more useful.

In the classroom, teachers use their plan books and other resources for data entry material. The following three critical areas must be entered initially:

1. **Content**. The subject matter itself, which includes critical concepts, facts, events, and focal works of literature or key case studies (Jacobs, 2001).

2. **Skills**. Action verbs that describe what the students did to learn the content, not what the teacher did. Skills can be assessed, observed, and described in specific terms. Skills are unlike general processes (Jacobs, 2001). It is helpful to have the list of verbs found in "Engine-Uity's Verbs and Products for Independent Study" folder (see Curriculum Mapping Resources Resources, p. 170).

3. **Assessments**. The major products and performances that are a demonstration of learning and are observable evidence of competence. Assessments are entered using nouns.

A good approach to helping teachers begin the data entry process is to have one of your support team members illustrate the process by entering data from his or her own

---

| **Fig. 6.4** | **10 Steps to Curriculum Mapping** |

1. Consult your lesson plan book to retrieve data.

2. Determine the content or topics taught. Avoid using numbers such as Chapter 1 or Objective 4.2, because they are nondescriptive.

3. Record this information on your map in the correct box. If you are entering the data on the computer, you can make the boxes as large as needed.

4. Determine the skills or processes you taught. What did students have to do to learn the concepts (not the activities you used to deliver the piece)? Did they recite? Calculate? Demonstrate? Practice? Interview? Skills must be recorded by using VERBS. Refer to your guide, *Verbs and Products for Independent Study*, which is based on Bloom's taxonomy.

5. Record the skills on your map.

6. Record the types of assessment (products and performances) used. What did the students do to demonstrate learning? Tests or quizzes? Speeches? Labs? Skits? Types of assessment need to be recorded as NOUNS.

7. List only the type of assessment. You do not have to go into great detail. If you used a rubric for scoring the assessment, be sure to include it on your map.

8. Record resources by listing field trips, speakers, videos, software, and related literature that is not part of your basal or literature book. It is okay to leave this section blank if nothing fits.

9. Save your maps to your disk, and print out a hard copy each month.

10. Turn in a copy of your map printouts to _____ by _____ .

Source: Maryville High School, Maryville, Tennessee.

plan book and resources. Then have your teachers enter data as the principal and a member of the support team observe and respond to entries and questions. This process is also a good time to reaffirm the importance of honesty when entering data, because the maps are used to help students reach a higher level of success. One successful strategy that Dr. Jacobs uses is to ask teachers to name a child in one of their classes. She then places an empty chair in the front of the group and asks the teachers to address what they do to "the child" in the chair. This personalization emphasizes the importance of being honest in the data entry for the sake of each child.

Another good strategy used by the Darke County Educational Service Center in Ohio is to create a "Tool Kit for Mapping" in a CD-ROM format. It should contain sample

Fig. 6.5	A Few Do's and Don'ts of Curriculum Mapping

- **Do** your mapping by yourself. There is no collaboration at this point in the process.

- **Don't** list content as Chapter 1 or Objective 2.5, because readers of your map will have no idea of the concepts taught.

- **Do** use verbs to describe skills and nouns to identify types of assessment.

- **Don't** edit as you go. These maps are not an evaluation tool. They will not be a part of your evaluation folder. We hope that the maps will help us determine some schoolwide and department goals, which will help our students and staff and will make ours an even better school.

- **Do** enter your information at the end of each grading period during the first term, and turn in your map by the deadline. If a unit, a chapter, or a project extends into the next grading period, enter it again. For this reason, weeks 5 and 14 are listed twice on the template.

- **Don't** procrastinate! The longer you wait, the harder it will get!

- **Do** record your data in real time. We are using the diary approach to mapping, which means we are recording what has actually happened in the curriculum during those time frames. The other approach is called a projected map.

- **Don't** use the projected approach to mapping. We have to be consistent in the approach and the format we use.

- **Do** limit your information to the space provided. We anticipate one page per grading period. If you have questions, please do not hesitate to ask Curriculum Mapping Facilitators.

- **Don't** forget that the maps will not be used to evaluate you. Their purpose is to collect authentic information about what students actually experience in our curriculum.

Source: Maryville High School, Maryville, Tennessee.

formats and answers to many questions about the mapping process. You may want to consider creating your own guide to mapping in a CD-ROM format for teachers to use as a reference. Be sure to include the format your teachers will use to enter data, examples of how to enter data, and other aids that make the mapping process friendly and that show the way your system will implement the process.

Processing and Using Data, and Aligning the Standards

When teachers have completely entered data for an area of the curriculum, it is time to go through the three-step process for reviewing the maps. The first review of the maps helps teachers understand their use, and it relieves much of the apprehension they felt at the beginning of the process. The following three steps compose the review process (see Appendix 7 for read-through forms to record the review process).

Step 1: Teacher as Editor

Each teacher becomes an editor for the maps. The principal and support team first decide how to put the maps together for an efficient review. All maps should be available to all teachers. Remember: for this first read, teachers do not create a grade level or subject area map. Teachers should see this step as a "storewide inventory" in which they evaluate the curriculum that the school offers so

they can determine what they are doing, what they need to do less of, and what is missing. In "mappers" terminology, they must know what is redundant, where the gaps are, and what is going on that they didn't know about.

To make this step move faster, you should demonstrate how to review maps. You can create a few maps that contain redundancies and gaps. Then, use a form, similar to the one in Figure 6.6, to record data from the review.

High school teachers often ask if they need to read maps out of their subject area concentrations. The answer to this question is YES. As in the previous example from Maryville High School, the school did an admirable job of guiding its staff members through the first read-through (see Figure 6.7 for a description of the process used at Maryville High School).

The first step in the process involves individual work that prepares teachers to work together in small groups.

Step Two: Small Mixed-Group Review

This is a critical step in which teachers share their findings. The question that often arises is, "Why can't we have the secretary make a list of all our collective findings?" This approach is not good because the mixed-group review is the greatest experience in the processing steps. Teachers really discuss and share what they have found.

Fig. 6.6	First Read-Through Summary Form

This form will be used as a guideline to help you read through the curriculum maps for the first time. As you read the maps, it is important to focus on a few vital aspects dealing with the content and skills sections.

Directions: As you read through a series of maps, record the pertinent information under each of the categories below. Use the examples in each category as a guide.

Grade Level of Maps: _____   **Subject:** _____

Gaps Found	Where/What Grade
Ex. Fractions (One class teaches to 1/2, two classes teach to 1/8, and one made no mention of fractions)	4th
Ex. Two classes used "listed" as a skill, and two used "describe" for the content of steps of mealworm life cycle.	5th

Redundancies Found	Where/What Grade
Ex. Life cycle of butterflies	K–4
Ex. All grades used "identify" for the content of shapes	4–6

Points of Interest/Comments

Ex. Neat idea: using geometry to develop miniature golf hole designs in 10th grade geometry.

Source: Created by Dave Shellhaas, Darke County Educational Service Center, Greenville, Ohio.

While no changes are made at this time, the discussions are rich and interesting. The focus in the school is now on what is best for the children. Gaps and redundancies are acknowledged, and now that teachers have some data, they can work together to create a curriculum for the students.

The composition of these small groups should be decided upon by carefully looking at the dynamics of the staff. Groups should be made up of no more than six to eight teachers. The groups should be diverse and composed of teachers who do not work together each day. Someone in each group should be designated to record the data. The groups usually finish their review in an hour or two. When the groups have completed the list of their findings, collect the data. Combine the lists for use in Step Three.

Step Three: Large-Group Review

All staff members meet and examine the compilation of findings from the small groups. The principal and his or her support team should facilitate this session. (If the faculty is very large, it may be necessary to go to job-alike groups.) The faculty identifies areas that can be handled with relative ease. For those areas, decide who will work on the revisions and on a timetable for action. Other considerations involve identifying areas in which revisions require long-term planning and areas in which further research is needed.

Devise a plan to deal with such issues. Faculties generally see the need to quickly target their assessments. Therefore, this time is good for a targeted read-through of building-level assessments to determine if they reflect the group's content, skills, and standards.

It is also the time to address aligning the standards in the maps. Once teachers are aware of curriculum needs, they develop consensus maps. Teachers in a grade level or subject area reach consensus on the content, skills, and assessments to which all students will have equal access. They also make sure the standards are inserted, and they note areas of need while seeking information on how to better achieve the standards. All teachers then use the maps the following year as they plan. Individual maps continue to be developed by teachers. Mapping is a process that never ends.

Note that while most maps have months of the year at the top, the placement does not mean that all teachers must teach the content and skills at the same time. The art of teaching is still alive and well. The initial phases of mapping reveal the science of teaching. Using these data to write good units and courses is the art of teaching. These consensus maps are good for only one year; because all students will have equal access to content, skills, and other areas, they will be better prepared when moving to the next grade level.

At this point, consider forming some expert study groups within your school. The following are examples of how these groups might work:

• **Assessment group.** Teachers in this group research and develop ways to design viable performance assessments. They learn to use data to improve text design and to meet the level of standards.

• **Vocabulary group.** Teachers review maps to determine if the vocabulary in the maps is consistent with the vocabulary in the standards and state testing examples. If it is not, this is an area of concern.

• **Learning behavior skills group.** This group might study *Habits of Mind: A Development Series* (Costa & Kallick, 2000) to help them develop a plan for integrating behavior skills in most unit designs.

• **Integration of curriculum group.** This group works on a way to use maps to write integrated units. When all maps of a grade level or interdisciplinary team are compiled, ideas for integrated units seem to pop out.

As the staff of CSLA began to write units, they decided to create an integrated map that chronicles in simple terms an outline for content and how the subject areas are integrated. Those maps are posted on the wall outside each classroom and are also sent home to parents to help them see the road map showing where teachers planned to take their children over the course of the year. The maps are wonderful public relations tools.

Using data to improve student learning is the reason curriculum maps are developed. It is critically important that teachers analyze the collected data. Principals need to lead their staff members toward an understanding of how to use the data; therefore, the principal needs to understand their use. It may be important for you as principal to seek out training on how to use the state's data and on effective strategies for supporting your staff in using the data.

As teachers use mapping data, ask questions, such as the following:

• What might be some possible targets for instruction?

• What do we need to look for in the maps to help us understand our results?

• What can we find out about the types of assessments we need?

• How might we place weightings on different types of assessments?

• How can different types of assessments work in our school?

• What school-level benchmark tests can we design that will match our standards?

For additional ideas to help you use the maps, see *Habits of Mind: A Developmental Series* (Costa & Kallick, 2000).

Principals should also seek out research to help teachers answer their questions on upgrading their expertise. Read and reflect with other teachers or principals about new findings. Form a support group with other principals or teachers to seek out information on how to improve teacher performance. One teacher said, "It is the teachers' behavior that has made a difference in our students' levels of performance, and curriculum mapping is the vehicle that led us to see where our performances were lacking."

When teachers work at higher levels of expertise, students also work at higher levels. Teachers worked in isolation before they came together to do curriculum mapping. Communication is the key to success. Marilyn Chapman, guidance counselor at CSLA, made the following comment:

> Curriculum mapping shattered the glass ceiling of teaching in isolation. It moved us toward clear communication, meaningful connections, and understanding of the power of professional collaboration that truly made a difference—not just in our instruction, but even more in our students—as growing lifelong learners. They began to see the "connections" too!

| Fig. 6.7 | **Maryville High School's Guide to Curriculum Map Reading** |

10 Steps to Curriculum Map Reading

The completion of the data collection stage of the mapping process is the end of the beginning. Our maps are good, but they are not yet as good as they can and will be. The purpose of the all-faculty review phase is to collect information from teachers who have different areas of expertise and who can provide a different perspective. Mapping is the equivalent of a storewide inventory. The success of this endeavor relies heavily on everyone's willingness to be involved.

As you read and review, pretend that you are a parent or that you are teaching this course for the first time. Ask yourself if the maps tell you what we expect our students to know, when they learn it, and what they do to show what they know. Remember that you do not have to understand course-specific terminology to understand and be able to follow the map. You are not expected to analyze in depth. Seven other professionals are reading the same set of maps, and the collective wisdom gathered during the discussions on February 19 will provide each grade or department valuable information. You will not be graded on this assignment, but you do have to turn it in!

Step One	Spend about **6–8 minutes** (really!) reading each map so you can complete Part One of the review process. Read the content section first. When something strikes you as a *Wow!* jot it down in the first section.
Step Two	Read the map from top to bottom in each column—content to assessment. Is it clear to you how students practice to gain proficiency and how they demonstrate what they know? Record your questions and comments in the **Analysis** section.
Step Three	If you see how something in this course can be connected to something you know about in another area of the curriculum, make note of it on the map so the appropriate department becomes aware of this possibility. If nothing strikes you, don't worry about it.
Step Four	Read the assessment section per course (18 weeks), and check off the types you found on the map. You do **not** need to tally the number of times each type of assessment occurred.
Step Five	List any use of technology that you found while reading each map.
Step Six	What confused you as a reader who is unfamiliar with this area of the curriculum? How might this map be improved? Do you have any questions or suggestions? Your input is valid and valuable.
Step Seven	Cross-comparisons: Read the maps again for the same course (English I, for example), and note any gaps you see or any questions you have. In your opinion, are essential elements being addressed in a comparable way?
Step Eight	Now read the maps of courses in sequence (English AP, 1, 2, 3, 4, for example), and jot down any repetitions or redundancies you notice or any questions you have.

(continued)

Fig 6.7	**Maryville High School's Guide to Curriculum Map Reading (*cont.*)**

Step Nine — Devote no more than 1 hour in steps 7 and 8. Remember that you are not working alone. Rule of thumb: No one should spend more than a total time of 3 to 4 hours on the read-review phase.

Step Ten — Take two aspirins, and contact David Messer in the morning or Mary Driskill anytime after 10:00 a.m. if you have questions or need more forms.

Schedule for Monday, February 19

8:30–10:00 — Your time to finish work on the reading-review process for your content area. Please bring your completed packet to the first session: the set of maps, an information sheet (Part One) attached to each map in the packet, and your comments and questions about possible gaps or redundancies (Part Two). **At the end of the day, the group facilitator will collect your packet, and all the information gathered during both sessions will be given to the appropriate department at a later date.**

10:00–12:00 — Morning discussion session: gathering information in each of the seven sections: learning connections between content and skills, possible areas for integration, types of assessment, use of technology, perceived learning gaps, perceived redundancies, and wows!

12:00–1:30 — Lunch

1:30–3:30 — Afternoon discussion session: clarifying ideas, recording and clarifying recommendations, ranking recommendations, and collecting packets.

Locations for Discussion Teams

Arts	370 (Byerley)	Glenda Anderson	Lisa Paine
English	366 (Jabbour)	Karin Papenhausen	Robin Castleman
Foreign Language	236 (King)	Teresa LeQuire	Becky Rhodes
Math	336 (Myers)	Liz Crawford	Alan Fair
PE/Wellness/Drivers Ed.	332 (Pickle)	Cathy Finney	Kevin Huffstetler
Science	235 (Roop)	Kaye Buckley	Karyn Brinks
Social Studies	336 (Weaver)	Jesse Robinette	Jody Ellis
Special Education	367 (Webb)	Kim Swann	Trisha Wilhoit

Source: Maryville High School, Chattanooga, Tennessee.

Sustaining the Process: Forming and Using Site-Based Councils

Create a site-based review council as soon as your staff has mapped and processed a curriculum area. This council provides the opportunity to sustain the work of mapping. One teacher said the council helps "institutionalize" the process. Teachers realize that mapping is not a one-shot curriculum study. The council fosters communication in the school, among and between schools, and serves as a liaison to the district council.

The school council meets regularly. Many schools meet at least four times each year, while others meet as the need arises. Many councils meet a week before school opens to train new staff members on every aspect of mapping and to pass on the yearly maps to the next level of study. The council makes sure that the yearly maps still spiral and that growth is occurring. If growth is not occurring, the council begins to find out why and makes plans for renewal. The council prepares for the year by looking at the data that have been gathered and by making a time line for implementing plans for the year. It is also wise for councils to plan to meet several times during the year to discuss any issues that have surfaced about curriculum and instruction.

The council members need to be selected using a job description. Members can rotate by serving for a period of one, two, or three years. This rotation ensures that new members learn from the more experienced members. Because many teachers feel overused, this pattern also ensures a rotation of responsibilities. The council focuses on staff development, and council meetings should be open to all staff members.

Once a working council is in place, the staff can continue with its mapping and renewal work whether there is a new principal or not. The teachers now have ownership in this work. They develop the curriculum, rather than implementing a given curriculum using an old model. Becky Malone, a teacher in Chattanooga, Tennessee, made the following observation:

> Curriculum mapping empowered me to "teach." It allowed me to be reflective in my planning. It became an avenue for me to have productive planning sessions with teachers who send me students and with the teachers I send students to. Curriculum mapping offered a road map for a successful school year for all my students.

In conclusion, my advice to principals is to stay the course. Your skills as an administrator and your teachers' skills as instructional leaders will grow. You and your teachers will create an enhanced teaching and learning environment based on the needs of the students.

7 Curriculum Mapping and Software

Creating an Information System for a Learning Community

Bena Kallick and James M. Wilson III

Now that we are working in a standards-based environment with high stakes associated with accountability, we can no longer do business as usual. The design of curriculum is more closely associated with assessment results than in previous years. Such realities demand more flexibility and speed as we manage information and greater interaction among educators to enhance systems for learning. The current wave of innovation in technology is providing tools to make curriculum dynamic and more easily revised. No dominant design has emerged from among the many developers. Technologists are learning from educators, and educators are learning from technologists in this ongoing cooperative evolution. However, many reasonable solutions do exist.

Technology and mapping are the perfect partners for creating, storing, and sharing information about curriculum, instruction, and assessment. Curriculum mapping collects the individual work of teachers in each classroom. Technology brings that individual work to the group level where it can be shared and where teachers can learn about innovative and successful practices and can make necessary revisions based on an analysis of performance data. This process of making work explicit and shared among individual teachers is referred to as "knowledge creation" (Nonaka & Takeuchi, 1995; Boisot, 1998). What is implied is that new knowledge about teaching and learning is created by bringing what has previously been tacit to an individual to a more explicit public dialogue. Knowledge creation recognizes the continuous process of how organizational knowledge is renewed by shared learning among members of an organization. In education, that knowledge finds its articulation explicitly and publicly in the curriculum. Such dynamism suggests that we need to replace the notion that "We have already *mapped* our curriculum" with "We are continuously *mapping* our curriculum."

Given the amount of information that comprises maps and the dynamism of knowledge creation, mapping without technology is an unwieldy experiment leading to myriad papers that limit rather than enhance the analysis of data. Fortunately, mapping with appropriate technology and organizational processes can be an evolutionary system of knowledge creation par excellence.

Using Software to Make the Mapping Process More Effective and Efficient

It is not difficult to observe the power of the mapping process through the conversations that teachers share about their individual interpretations of curriculum. Teachers, sitting with maps in hand, discuss what and how they teach. Such a process promotes teacher conversations across grade levels and across schools. It is not unusual to hear a teacher say, "I had no idea that you were doing that in your classroom," or "How do you do that in your classroom?" Those professional conversations create a natural condition for the evolution of knowledge about the most successful practices for improving student learning.

Teachers have long complained about the isolation of the classroom. They know they need to work together, but the prevalent reality is that the school day is not currently designed for those important conversations. At best, planning time equates to the immediacy of the moment, not to the long view of the year or to the multiple years that students spend in school. When teachers do not know the sequence of the curriculum across students' years of schooling, students have a disjointed experience. Rather than each year's work resting on the work of the previous year, students often experience each year as a new event. When state tests define a single year to benchmark performance, the problem is exacerbated. Preparation for a 4th grade math test, for example, requires coordinated preparation in grades K–4. It takes an integrated K–12 curriculum to develop students' capabilities so they meet high school exit standards. The compounding influence of education on a student's cumulative knowledge requires tools to enhance and understand how numerous teachers act over time as a team to cultivate that knowledge.

Curriculum mapping is a means for developing such a coordinated curriculum. Dr. Heidi Hayes Jacobs (1997a) outlined phases for a successful mapping process in Chapter 2 of her book, *Mapping the Big Picture: Integrating Curriculum and Assessment K–12*. Her phases use the paradigm of knowledge creation by promoting steps that transform the tacit knowledge of individual classroom teachers into an explicit organizational knowledge. Jacobs assumes that software should be used, in contrast to generating their maps by hand, in print.

Moving from Printed Maps to a Shared Database

Let's consider the developmental stages that a district might go through to make a transition from hand-written to shared database. Figure 7.1 shows the steps in turning handwritten maps into computer-based ones and identifies the reports that the database makes available.

Stage One: Making the Transition from Print to Computer

Stage One is composed of two phases that help teachers transition from print to computer:

Phase 1: Collecting the Data. When introducing technology, we must be aware that not all teachers are tech savvy—in fact, we might characterize some as technophobic. Because the main purpose is to have teachers develop an initial knowledge of the process of creating maps, we suggest that you start by handwriting map entries. However, to enhance a subsequent transition to technology, the templates for creating the handwritten maps should mirror the format of the software. These maps are brought to the first read-through. There should be no barriers to getting started. Until the process of mapping itself is understood, technology can be an unnecessary burden to learning. The handwriting of the maps achieves the aim of transforming their tacit practices into explicit language. This first step, shown in Figure 7.2, might be considered a quick first draft.

Phase 2: Completing the First Read-Through. The first read-through opens the door for integrating software into the mapping process. During the first read-through, the map will be revised. In every subsequent meeting, both the maps and the process of creating maps requires further revisions. As teachers gain a better understanding of the elements to put into the maps (content, skills, assessments, and essential questions) and of how those elements are interrelated, they will be motivated to revise their maps.

Mapping software is designed, in part, to collect mapping elements—such as essential questions, contents, skills, and assessments—and to compose such elements into maps. If the software is well designed, its purpose will be to provide a shared and searchable database of elements and maps. This capability to share has an immediate payoff during this initial data entry process. For example, teachers who are teaching a common course of study have immediate access to maps and map elements from their colleagues. Through a search function, teachers can see other teachers' maps from other courses of study. In other words, communication is mediated electronically, and

---

Fig. 7.1   **Curriculum Revision Continuum**

Stage 1: Making the Transition from Print to Computer
1. Each individual teacher creates a curriculum by entering data into software or hard copy that mirrors the software.
2. The first read-through yields two reports: one showing the frequency counts of content and skills and another showing the alignment to standards.

Stage 2: Building Consensus Maps
1. A mixed-group review report by building, department, and course is generated.
2. A large-group review report with alignment by course and department is yielded.

Stage 3: Using Assessment Data to Inform Decisions
Long-term research and development is facilitated by the generation of reports of assessment types, units, and lessons that consolidate data within departments and courses.

---

through that medium, mapping becomes a dynamic collaboration. Educators no longer need to wait until the next staff development session for an opportunity to observe and understand the contributions of their colleagues.

Stage Two: Building Consensus Maps

The first stage of development has led teachers through the following:

• Documenting what takes place in their classrooms

• Participating in important conversations about continuity across grades and subjects

• Moving from individual teaching knowledge to group knowledge

Technology can transform the traditional work of the curriculum committee into a network organizational structure where information is transferred at different times and from a wider range of participants. Maps in database form provide regular, consistent, and efficient information about what is taking place in the classroom. Reports from such a database provide the following ongoing information:

• How the frequency of contents is addressed

Fig. 7.2	**Sample Curriculum Map: First Draft**

Teacher: _Matt Russell_   **Course:** _ELA: Reading_   **Section:** _4th Grade_   **Year:** _2002–2003_

	October	**November**	**December**
Essential Questions	What is the difference between nonfiction and fiction? In what way does a biography tell a story?	How do writers "hook" their readers? What is a document-based question?	How did E. B. White "hook" readers? How can we explain the fact that White's work continues to engage readers?
Content	Biographies: a range of books available for different levels of reading. Students choose independent reading.	Author's hooks: literary devices, plot structures, openings that engage. Political cartoons.	Metaphors, similes, and analogies; *Charlotte's Web*
Skills	Identifying points of view; distinguishing fact from opinion	Identifying opening lines and titles; writing practice on engaging the reader	Identifying metaphors, similes, and analogies; using metaphors, similes, and analogies
Assessment Type	Research paper demonstrating understanding of the work; spelling test	Three-author essay—students will identify three authors of their choice and employ corresponding hooks	Identifying key metaphors, similes, and analogies in a chapter of *Charlotte's Web*; interpreting the novel

• How the skills are associated with the content

• How the standards are being addressed

As Joyce Dwyer, a principal in Ellington, Connecticut, commented:

Using the software has moved our mapping initiative forward. We are now talking with one another with far greater precision. Our suggestions for revision are based on data, an exciting way to bring the faculty past personalities and into thoughtful decisions.

This thoughtfulness emerges from better access to information that has been generated by creating reports to inform educators about the nature of the mapping process in their district and by providing tools to select best practices from among the range of educators' creative efforts.

Phase 3: Mixed-Group Review. As Dr. Jacobs (1997a) suggests, it is useful to create discussion groups composed of teachers who do not usually work together. Particular subjects become subcultures with a shared point of view that is based on the idiosyncrasies of their conception of knowledge. It is well known that innovation often occurs when practitioners from different disciplines or cultures interact on a project. The mixed-group review for mapping uses this approach to promote innovation in organizations. Such groups are able to look at the maps with fresh eyes. Because participants are not as close to the details of the map in a particular grade or subject, they can raise questions that teachers closer to the details may easily overlook. A mixed group can reveal what is tacit within particular subjects and grades, as members seek clarification on the "short-hand" of that culture with its unquestioned traditions and practices. To best facilitate discussion, the groups should consist of mixed grades and departments and should be no larger than six to eight members.

The use of well-designed software transforms the conversations by making explicit the elements in individual maps and the patterns and trends among many maps. For example, teachers can obtain a report of all the contents, skills, and essential questions for a particular grade level and the frequency with which they occur in maps. By looking at such reports over several grades, the teachers can observe both the scope and the sequence of the elements. In this way, educators can study the learning journey of a student from one course to the next and from one year to the next.

Processing the information produces new knowledge about the curriculum for group discussions. For example, Figure 7.3 lists some questions that might guide the discussions and focus the editing process.

Next, look at the report shown in Figure 7.4 that was generated from the data that teachers put into their individual maps. It shows a consolidated report across all 5th grade English Language Arts teachers in the district.

Teachers assessing these data could ask, "What are the content and skills that matter?" Their editing question might be, "Among the unique elements, are there ones we should consider for our essential curriculum?"

What has technology brought to this phase? It has provided a means to bring the individual work of teachers to the group level by summarizing the data into special categories and by showing how frequently such elements are used in maps. Drawing on this information, curriculum review can then proceed to create a consensus curriculum—what we expect all students to know and be able to do for particular courses of study.

Phase 4: Large-Group Review. Each phase represents an ever-increasing number of teachers conversing about curriculum. Therefore, the conversation provides an increase in perspectives that can unravel the tacit knowledge in the organization and can diffuse what is learned among an ever-widening audience. The large-group review should include either the entire faculty of a school or the faculty of a department across grades K–12. Once again, reports can elevate such conversations. For example, a report can show where the curriculum is aligned

---

Fig. 7.3 | **Questions to Guide Editing**

What content and skills are in the maps *within* a grade level?

Editing questions:
- Do we all agree on which content and skills are important?
- Do the elements we observe constitute a part of what we will eventually call our essential curriculum?
- What content and skills are shown *across* grade levels?
- Do we observe a repetition or a spiraling of complexity for particular elements?
- What is the frequency of essential questions, contents, and skills in maps within a particular course or grade?
- What are the unique contents and skills?
- Are we observing synonyms or unique elements?
- Can we begin to develop a common language?

---

with standards and where it is not. Such a report provides a rich opportunity to discuss revision. The following questions can help focus the discussion:

- What do we need to add to address the standards?
- What might we need to drop out so that we can make this standard important?
- Are all standards of equal weight?

Stage 3: Using Assessment Data to Inform Decisions

This final stage incorporates long-term planning through research and development.

Phase 5: Long-Term Research and Development. One of the predicted outcomes of the mapping process is that organizational structures change as this process ensues (see Jacobs, 1997a, Chapter 6). This outcome occurs as a result of all teachers sharing and

revising their work in a public forum, rather than, for example, a representative group of teachers making curriculum revisions in a summer workshop. As the conversations about teaching and learning become more widely shared, the culture moves from isolated classroom interpretations of the educational process to a collective understanding about what we must address for consistency and continuity across all classrooms. This approach does not mean that teachers lose their individuality and creativity as a result of making their work public. Rather, it means that there is a professional community of learning in which practice is examined in light of a set of standards, and successful practices are recognized and made accessible for adoption or adaptation by all teachers. This sharing leads to "mapping with precision" as uncertainties are addressed and practices are refined during a professional

Fig. 7.4	**Curriculum Map Data Report**

Course: *Reading/Language 5*   **Year:** *2002–2003*

Essential Questions	Number of Teachers Using the Element	Total Teachers	Percentage of Total Teachers
What makes a community work together?	2	53	3.77
Why are we studying penguins?	1	53	1.89
Why are penguins black and white?	1	53	1.89
How is a classroom community like our Barrington community?	2	53	3.77
How does character count in building a community?	1	53	1.89
Why does Cindy dislike penguins?	1	53	1.89
What are our roles as citizens in the world?	1	53	1.89
How can I share myself in my writing?	2	53	3.77
Why would people want to be judged by their peers?	1	53	1.89
What exactly is a peer?	1	53	1.89
Why are my feelings important?	1	53	1.89
Content	**Number of Teachers Using the Element**	**Total Teachers**	**Percentage of Total Teachers**
Writing	2	53	3.77
Language Arts Concepts—2. Punctuation	1	53	1.89
Language Arts Concepts—6. Acquiring, Assessing, and Communicating Info	2	53	3.77
Language Arts Concepts—7. Speaking	2	53	3.77
Language Arts Concepts—8. Listening	1	53	1.89
Community	2	53	3.77
Listening and Speaking: Speaking Skills and Strategies	1	53	1.89

(continued)

Fig. 7.4	Curriculum Map Data Report (*cont.*)		
Content	**Number of Teachers Using the Element**	**Total Teachers**	**Percentage of Total Teachers**
Literary Genres: Fantasy	1	53	1.89
Literary Genres: Narrative	1	53	1.89
Reading Skills: Author's Purpose and Perspective	1	53	1.89
Reading Skills: Fact and Opinion	2	53	3.77
Reading Skills: Identifying Main Idea	1	53	1.89

dialogue driven by open inquiry. The process creates a forum for educators to raise questions. Because the curriculum used in classrooms is explicit, data to answer questions might be obtained through the use of reports generated by the software.

For example, we can study the data entered in the maps regarding assessment types. We can see a report that looks at that data course by course, such as the following:

• The number of teachers in the district who teach the course

• The number of times teachers have reported using that assessment type

• The percentage of use represented for a department or a grade

Teachers within a department or grade may meet to discuss whether students have ample opportunities to demonstrate what they know. Although we may espouse the need for multiple assessments that provide different kinds of demonstrations of learning, we may find that the assessment types are very limited. The first questions we need to ask are about the integrity of the data. The questions might include, "Did all teachers enter all their assessments?" and "How do we understand the data we see?"

Figure 7.5 shows an example of a report on assessment types.

Another critical analysis of a particular test may show a range of performance in the state math test. An item analysis could show that students do not do well with problem solving. Teachers can then return to their maps and observe that problem solving is listed every year from grades 1 through 4. However, they do not list what they specifically do to teach problem solving. To know more, the conversation must become more specific in its inquiry. The following questions can guide this discussion:

• On which strategies do we focus for instruction?

• When do we teach students how to explain their reasoning?

Fig. 7.5	Sample Report on Assessment Types	
Assessment Type	**Number of Assessments**	**Percentage of All Assessments**
Creative writing	1	2.1
Performance	1	2.1
Essay	3	6.4
Essay of narrator	1	2.1
Essay of character	5	10.6
Essay of theme	1	2.1
Final exam	2	4.3
Outline	1	2.1
Personal essay	2	4.3
Presentation	1	2.1
Projects	1	2.1
Quiz	15	31.9
Research	2	4.3
Rhetorical analysis	1	2.1
Scrapbook	1	2.1
Self-assessment	1	2.1
Text explication	3	6.4
Unit test	4	8.5
Worksheet	1	2.1

• What graphic organizers are introduced, and when are they introduced?

• What is introduced as a beginning concept?

• When do we expect that students will have sufficient understanding of the concept?

• What constitutes repetition, and what constitutes spiraling?

Conversations to answer such questions always lead to greater precision in thinking. The assessment results can be cautiously used to examine the alignment of curriculum and assessments to determine whether elements in the assessments are not covered in the curriculum or elements in the curriculum are not covered in the assessments. The former may lead to lower scores; the latter may complement understanding or may, on scrutiny, be frivolous. This kind of scrutiny raises important questions about curriculum, and the maps provide the requisite data to address such questions.

Meeting Challenges for Bringing Mapping and Technology into Schools

We see four critical challenges that need to be addressed as schools seek to become 21st-century learning communities. The following section identifies each challenge and provides corresponding recommendations.

Challenge One: Understanding the Illusion of Instant Gratification

Although the promise of a paperless, electronic world is that we will be more efficient, the truth is that technologies are still rather quirky. Certainly, we have all had the experience of doing work on the computer that ends up taking longer than it would have without technology because of the learning curve required to become proficient on the computer. In addition, many teachers are not comfortable using technology. Using mapping software may be their first computer experience. They are now confronted with two changes in the way they think about teaching: (1) they must document in a map what they address from month-to-month, and (2) they must learn to use a piece of software.

To transition to the use of technology so we can enhance organizational processes, we need to develop the training and technical support systems needed to successfully implement information technology. We also need to develop realistic expectations about the rate of implementation of such a process. Impulsive use of technology and of mapping implementation without real understanding is doomed to failure. Some good tools exist in the market, but there is no panacea. All tools take learning, testing, resource planning for training and support, and the sagacity and skill of cautious and careful implementation.

Challenge Two: Building a Culture for Collaborative Work

Knowledge creation requires trust. To articulate work and to share it with others require an environment that appreciates such efforts and that provides support, both to constructively criticize such efforts and to recognize exemplary work. As we all know, teachers are not accustomed to open dialogue that encourages skepticism and critical inquiry. Too often, conversations are intentionally focused on harmony, albeit false harmony. If we are to do serious work that requires eliminating some curriculum, adding new curriculum, or moving curricular requirements from one grade to another, we need to have data-based conversations.

We must learn how to have such conversations without fear of peer or administrative evaluations. The information provided as a result of data put into the software gives teachers an opportunity to develop the skills of thoughtful dialogue. The challenge is to build relationships among professionals who have a sufficient degree of trust to learn together. The sharing of maps is often the first public documentation of what teachers are addressing in their classrooms, which is a major change for most schools and is central to making the best use of mapping and technology.

Challenge 3: Organizing the Data

School districts with site-based management have left it to individual schools to make sense of each school's issues without a systemic view of the district's issues. Thus, at the level of data collection, this independence may have spawned disparate kinds of data elements, formats, identification numbers, and codes. Such diversity is anathema to databases at the integrated enterprise level. A Tower of Babel has been innocently created.

The value of a shared database is that teachers share their work across courses, grades, and departments. This sharing requires a process of "cleansing" the data of such differences. In many districts, this is the first time that teachers have been asked for

coherence and consistency across all schools. As schools depend more and more on information technology, this much-needed systemic, rather than site-based, perspective must prevail in terms of data and information.

Challenge 4: Knowing What We Need to Know

The promise of information technology has brought more tasks than we know how to handle. We have requests for numerous reports from our state departments of education. Yet, when we try to understand what the report really should contain, we find a set of "inarticulate demands" (Hamel & Prahalad, 1994). That is, we know we need or want something, but we cannot say precisely what it is. This confusion is a common phenomenon when a new technology emerges. For example, we may not like a user interface, but we can't describe what would be better. We know the report just printed is not what we want, but we cannot describe what we really need.

Another example of this ambiguity is when we are asked to make certain that our curriculum is aligned with standards. When we unpack that request, the following questions might arise:

• Does this ambiguity mean that the content that teachers teach should be aligned with standards?

• Does this confusion mean that the skills the teachers address should be aligned with standards?

• Are we concerned with how frequently the contents and skills are addressed over time or within a school year?

• Are we asking about all standards or just the ones that correlate with state tests?

In other words, we recognize the need for alignment, but we are uncertain which elements are aligned with which standards. Again, we call these inarticulate demands, because we don't yet know what reports will work within our organization. The answer to these questions emerges from trial and error or from a report we have yet to imagine. Ultimately, we must be pragmatic. We need to keep reminding ourselves that we are seeking such information to help our students. It is at this point where tenacity and belief play a key role, because it takes time for the inarticulate demand to find its solution in an innovation.

The best software solutions emanate from companies that have deep knowledge of education and that have sought leaders who can help define those demands in meaningful ways, both for the districts and for the state education departments. One of the most significant issues in choosing software from a vendor is the depth of educational expertise and technological expertise, plus the integration between those two levels of expertise that is brought to bear on adapting technology to the work of educators.

The Vision and Requirements of Mapping

Mapping software can become the medium of organizational memory, the mechanism for diffusion of practices, and an archive of the best curriculum assets. Teachers can share elements (essential questions, contents, skills, assessments, lessons, units) and entire maps. Through the selection and retention of superior essential questions, contents, skills, assessments, and lessons, the system can naturally evolve and converge toward best practices. In addition, successful practices from experts in the field can inoculate the database and easily diffuse elements of it among teachers. In such cases, the software can marshal contagion in a positive way to rapidly spread these practices within the district.

Success in mapping requires these practices:

• Knowledge of mapping and its process
• Appropriate technology
• Appropriate organizational culture to engage in constructive inquiry

Implementing mapping in a district requires the capability to recognize the district's strengths and weaknesses. The next step is to develop a clear plan to obtain and deploy the expertise and resources as everyone faces the challenges inherent in implementing mapping. The procurement and the management of expertise and resources to implement mapping require strong leadership in the district. The leaders must hold a clear, long-range vision of mapping while methodically, carefully, and tenaciously imparting new knowledge and new technology and while fostering a culture of inquiry among district educators.

It is important to understand that these responsibilities are the ones districts must assume, in conjunction with their vendors, to make mapping and technology work. The payoff of this undertaking is a practical synthesis of the science of teaching with the art of teaching. Creativity and knowledge are united and shared in a community of educational practitioners. A professional community of learning emerges that inspires new teachers, renews those who have been teaching for some time, and finally provides real information to ensure that a student has a coherent educational experience about grades and subjects.

Curriculum Mapping in Alternative Education Settings

Joseph Lachowicz

Teachers in alternative education settings benefit enormously from the process of curriculum mapping. Our experience with 11 distinctive alternative education populations in Pittsburgh, Pennsylvania, underscores the benefits. We chose curriculum mapping as the vehicle for constructing curriculum and using assessment data because it has proven to be consistent and it meets the needs of teachers and students. Curriculum mapping provides the most effective staff development as we create meaningful lessons and experiences for our alternative education students, including those with special needs.

When we began our search to determine the best format for writing curriculum across our diverse programs, we considered the following questions:

• How do we write a curriculum for a population that changes daily?

• What should be taught to students who may be in school for only one week?

• Because students are enrolled from various districts, what curriculum is acceptable to all districts?

• How will planning be accomplished?

• Do teachers discuss curriculum, or do they work in isolation?

With our diverse and ever-changing population, we needed some consistency in our curriculum. We discussed a computer-based curriculum, but it lacked the much-needed personalized instruction for our population. Adopting the curriculum of one of our school districts was a possible remedy. However, because we serve 42 districts, it would be difficult to decide which district's curriculum would best meet our student's needs. Teachers must have some autonomy about their curriculum. Therefore, the curriculum should be based on the students currently in placement. After much dialogue and extensive research, we chose curriculum mapping as the solution to the challenges our teachers faced. By reading, studying, and attending workshops on curriculum mapping, we found it easy to discern the significance, relevance, and functionality of curriculum maps.

Background

The Alternative Education Program (AEP) is a branch of the Allegheny Intermediate Unit No. 3 in Pittsburgh, Pennsylvania. Our mission is to provide quality instruction and counseling to students in a supportive, technology-rich environment. Students enrolled in the AEP are affiliated with Juvenile Court and the Children, Youth, and Families (CYF) Agency, both in Allegheny County.

CYF is a child welfare agency whose mission is to protect children from abuse and neglect, to preserve families, and to provide permanent and safe homes for children. Students who are affiliated with CYF and who are not able to attend their home school can receive their education through one of the AEP schools.

The AEP consists of 11 countywide programs with 80 staff members serving approximately 4,000 students each year. The program provides educational services in three distinct settings: the shelter system, the detention system, and the community-based system. The courts place students in the shelter and detention systems; parents, school districts, probation officers, and children and youth workers refer students to the community-based programs.

Shelter Systems

The AEP administers three shelter schools: two programs for middle and secondary students and one for elementary students. Those three sites are located in various communities throughout the county. Shelter programs, as well as other alternative education programs, are created on the basis of the needs of CYF and Juvenile Court. The programs are operated in a nonsecure institutional setting.

Shelter programs are short-term educational programs that provide 5 full days of instruction for students, because they are not able to attend their home district while in placement. The average stay for such students is 30 days, but they can be enrolled anywhere from 1 day to 3 months. Approximately 1,000 students pass through the shelter system each year.

Each shelter site has a staff of four to seven people and serves approximately 20 to 40 students daily. Because new students are enrolled and released daily, enrollments constantly change. Parental visits, doctor appointments, court hearings, and alternative placement visits are other factors that cause the student population to fluctuate continuously. Students receive credit for their learning in the alternative education programs. All students in attendance for 20 days or more receive a transcript that is forwarded to their home district.

Detention Systems

The AEP provides services in two detention settings. Shuman Center School, which is located in the Shuman Detention Center, is a facility for juvenile delinquents. The Academic Institute, which is located inside the Allegheny County Jail, is for juveniles who have been certified as adults in criminal court. Inmates who are up to 21 years of age and are detained at the Allegheny County Jail are eligible for educational services.

Shuman Center School educates approximately 2,400 students each year with a staff of 17 teachers. Approximately 70 to 100 students attend school on a daily basis. The average stay for those students is 30 days. At the Academic Institute, approximately 500 students are educated each year, with an average stay of 45 days. Six teachers are assigned to the Academic Institute program.

Community Schools East and West

The community schools are long-term alternative programs for students who are in grades 9 through 12 and who are unable to adjust to their local public schools. Students are enrolled in the school located near their home district. Court-affiliated students attend at no cost to the district. A small number of noneligible students attend on a fee-for-service basis.

Students at the community school earn credits related to their home district's graduation requirements. A Memorandum of Understanding stating that the home district accepts all earned credits is signed. Students are evaluated for continued enrollment on a semester basis. Data show that students who attend the community schools usually stay through graduation because of their success in a small environment. The enrollment ranges from 20 to 35 students each day. Each site has a staff of five to seven people.

The Mapping Process

Once curriculum mapping was chosen as our communication tool, dialogue began immediately. Teachers examined mapping's purpose, how it would be implemented, and what maps would look like. This decision took place at the end of a school year so teachers could implement mapping the following school year.

The First Year

The story of our work in the first year describes our initial expectations, emerging time lines, map evaluations, and our reflections.

Expectations

At the beginning of the new school year, teachers attended training on how to write curriculum maps and what format they would use. In the early stages of implementation, the idea was to help teachers become familiar with writing maps. Unless technology is used to create maps, the process becomes an overwhelming task. Therefore, a basic computer format (see Figure 8.1) was developed so teachers could input their maps. The format is user friendly and includes prompts to input the necessary information for an effective curriculum plan.

During the first year, the emphasis was to align skills, activities, and assessments. What teachers wanted students to learn (skills) formed the basis for student assessment. Because it made sense for the entire picture of the lessons to be on one document, activities were also included in teacher maps. The activities were evaluated by teachers and administrators to determine whether teachers used various teaching strategies to help students learn skills. Even though standards were also listed on the maps, the main purpose at this time was to help teachers get accustomed to developing curriculum maps.

To help teachers develop this new process, two teachers from the Auberle shelter, Jessica Ohr and Jamie Ray, attended extensive training on curriculum mapping, including a national Curriculum Mapping Conference. Having teachers with extensive training was a tremendous help, because they could provide strong support to our teachers. Their expertise allowed teachers to seek help from peers, rather than just from administrators.

Time Lines

Schedules (see Figure 8.2) were developed to ensure time for reviewing maps by teacher teams and administrators. Teachers developed their maps one month at a time. Use of the technology made this task simpler and allowed teachers to cut and paste into the next month what was not covered in the previous month. Working in a one-month time period allowed teachers to focus their thinking on the immediate planning that was necessary and allowed administrators to review maps on an ongoing basis.

At the start of the school year while they were in training, the teachers used the diary approach for the month of September. A diary approach is a map written in real time and written in a more day-to-day approach as learning takes place. Because there was no time to plan before school opened in September, teachers wrote their maps as they taught each day.

As Figure 8.2 shows, team meetings were scheduled each month to discuss content. The team consisted of all teachers at each site, meaning all disciplines were included in the meeting, which allowed for dialogue and integration of those various disciplines. Although dialogue should occur constantly, one formal meeting was scheduled monthly

Fig. 8.1	Mapping Format

Subject:_____

Unit: _____ : _____   Instructor: _____
                                               Month: _____

Resources:

Standards:

Content	Skills	Activities	Assessments

Source: Allegheny Intermediate Unit, Allegheny, Pennsylvania.

to allow teachers time to discuss their ideas. Maps were submitted to administrators twice a month: at the beginning of the month to show what was planned, and at the beginning of the following month to show what was actually accomplished. As each month began, teachers were not required to list the activities. Instead, they were asked to concentrate more on what they wanted students to learn and on how they planned to assess the learning.

Evaluation of Maps

Of the 11 schools in our program, curriculum mapping was implemented in three sites. By starting with a smaller group of three, implementation of the concept was manageable for administrators, because they could read all of the maps. With only three sites, administrators had enough time to give adequate and frequent feedback to teachers.

Administrators analyzed the maps using the following questions for guidance:

• Are skills, activities, and assessments aligned?

• Is there evidence of integration among the disciplines?

• What instructional strategies are teachers implementing?

• What methods are teachers using to assess students?

Feedback from administrators is essential in mapping. Without feedback, teachers have no guidelines on how they are doing, whether they are improving, or whether they understand the concept. Feedback allows teachers to improve their lesson planning. In addition, reading maps provides administrators with an understanding of what each teacher is planning each month and helps administrators recognize which teachers are working to integrate their lessons. Mapping is intense work for both teachers and administrators.

Administrators also used maps in both formative and summative teacher evaluations. Although maps were not formally evaluated, they provided an excellent tool for administrators to use as they observed teachers. The observations provided an opportune time to provide feedback on the alignment between what was taught and what was shown on the maps.

During the first year, teachers were not required to include essential questions in their maps. Because essential questions are a difficult topic, it was felt that the demand on teachers would be overwhelming. However, what happened during the first year was pleasantly surprising. As the year progressed, teachers started writing questions in their maps for the content, skills, and activities planned. This addition led to discussions about what essential questions are, what their purposes are, and how they focus teaching. With this dialogue, teachers began to understand essential questions. This experience made implementing essential questions in the maps much easier during the following year.

Fig. 8.2	Curriculum Mapping Schedule Summary				
	CSE	**CSW**	**McK Ed**	**MEC**	**E-Lib**
Due to Team					
Discussed by Team					
Submitted to Administrator					
Updated & Completed	10/05/01	10/05/01	10/05/01	10/05/01	10/05/01
Submitted to Administrator	10/09/01	10/09/01	10/09/01	10/09/01	10/09/01
October	**CSE**	**CSW**	**McK Ed**	**MEC**	**E-Lib**
Due to Team	09/24/01	09/24/01	09/24/01	09/24/01	09/24/01
Discussed by Team	Week of 09/24/01				
Submitted to Administrator	10/01/01	10/01/01	10/01/01	10/01/01	10/01/01
Updated & Completed	11/05/01	11/05/01	11/05/01	11/05/01	11/05/01
Submitted to Administrator	11/07/01	11/07/01	11/07/01	11/07/01	11/07/01
November	**CSE**	**CSW**	**McK Ed**	**MEC**	**E-Lib**
Due to Team	10/25/01	10/25/01	10/25/01	10/25/01	10/25/01
Discussed by Team	Week of 10/29/01				
Submitted to Administrator	11/02/01	11/02/01	11/02/01	11/02/01	11/02/01
Updated & Completed	12/05/01	12/05/01	12/05/01	12/05/01	12/05/01
Submitted to Administrator	12/07/01	12/07/01	12/07/01	12/07/01	12/07/01

Thoughts About Year One

Because all programs, except at the Shuman Center School, are limited to a staff of four to seven people per site and because each teacher in a discipline teaches all subjects, we needed a map based on the population of each school. For example, the math teacher is teaching basic math, consumer math, algebra, and geometry. Students in the classes are at different grade levels and abilities. Therefore, it made the most sense to develop and use horizontal maps (see Figure 8.3, which shows how math learning takes place across the subjects for the learners).

For short-term students in alternative placements, using horizontal maps is much more efficient and effective than developing vertical maps (see Figure 8.4, which shows how math learning takes place from grade level to grade level).

Next, teachers met to develop interdisciplinary lessons. Teaming is critical for this development. If teachers do not work together, or if they work in isolation, mapping will not be successful. Then students will suffer because they are not being provided the best education. Although not all topics can be integrated, the maps allowed administrators to easily recognize when teachers did not try to integrate disciplines.

Obstacles encountered in the first year included determining whether some learning was a skill or an activity. For example, the standard of "Students will identify the components of a well-written letter" could easily be a skill or an activity. The determination is defined by an assessment; all skills are assessed. If letter writing is assessed, then it is considered to be a skill. If it is not assessed, it can be an activity if it aligns to the skill being taught. Another difficulty for some teachers was the actual alignment of skills, activities, and assessments. Feedback from administrators helped resolve this problem.

At the end of the first year, teachers were asked to complete an anonymous survey about their reactions to curriculum mapping. The results were extremely encouraging. A high percentage of teachers felt that writing maps provided an opportunity to really think about what they were teaching. They also felt that their teaching improved, their curriculum was more organized, and the maps were relevant to their teaching.

Teachers' comments included the following:

- "Mapping helped me focus."
- "Mapping helped with cross-curricular lessons."
- "Mapping provided an excellent translation from thinking to writing lesson plans and activities."

Map development during the first year was a learning process. The following list describes the time line of the first year:

- In-service training on curriculum mapping: Administrators explained the concept of mapping.
- Use of technology: A technology format was created to use when developing maps.

Fig. 8.3	**Math Map (Horizontal)**

Unit:	Instructor: _____ Month: _____

RESOURCES: *Integrated Math* textbook, *Applications in the Real World* textbook, Internet

STANDARDS:

2.2.11a   Develop and use computational concepts, operations, and procedures with real numbers in problem-solving situations.

2.3.11   Select and use appropriate units and tools to measure to the degree of accuracy required in particular measurement situations.

ESSENTIAL QUESTIONS: If two polygons have the same perimeter, are their areas the same?

Content	Skills	Activities	Assessments
• Area • Perimeter	• Use appropriate instruments and units for measuring area, perimeter. • Develop formulas and procedures for determining measurements. • Calculate the area and perimeter of objects.	• KWL on area and perimeter • Worksheet on www.eduhelper.com • Versatile manipulatives • Graphic organizer on area and perimeter and its properties • Comparison and contrast of area and perimeter • Given a length of fence, determining maximum area • Calculating the perimeter and area of various polygons	• Classroom exercises • Quiz • Rubric on properties of area on the graphic organizer • Scatter plot graph

• Skills, activities, and assessments: Administrators and teachers emphasized alignment among these areas.

• Schedule for the year: Due dates were set for submitting maps to administrators.

• Feedback: Administrators and teachers maintained continuous dialogue and formative evaluation of the maps.

• Self-evaluation: Teachers completed a survey to gather data about how they felt maps served as effective planning tools.

Teachers were required to develop only one map, even though they may have been teaching three different classes. Maps were not used as an evaluation tool. Administrators worked with teachers to learn how best to write maps, which, in turn, helped teachers in planning their lessons.

The Second Year

At the beginning of the second year, administrators introduced two more schools to curriculum mapping. The teachers involved during the first year proved that curriculum mapping could be successful with short-term students, thereby alleviating a concern expressed when mapping was first introduced.

Goals

Training on mapping continued throughout the second school year. Curriculum mapping videos were purchased, and all teachers were required to view the tapes. Dr. Heidi Hayes Jacobs provided a one-day workshop exclusively for the alternative education teachers, which allowed our teachers to discuss their concerns and experiences with mapping and to validate the work they were doing.

A new computer database was developed to make the mapping information much easier to read and understand. Because those who teach in the same content areas are located at various sites, it was difficult for them to work together. This new program, however, allowed teachers to search the database to find out what teachers of the same content areas were planning at other sites. It also allowed a search by either content area or skills. If, for example, someone wanted information on the Civil War, that teacher could type in those key words in the search function, and all maps with the words would be shown. This search tool not only allowed teachers to search other maps, but also allowed administrators to read all maps easily.

Fig. 8.4	Math Topical Map (Vertical)		
Month	**Grade 7**	**Grade 8**	**Grade 9**
September	Numbers, number systems, number relationships	Measurement, estimation	Mathematical reasoning, inductive and deductive reasoning
October	Problem solving with interpreting results	Statistics, data analysis	Probability, predictions
November	Geometry, shapes and their properties and principles	Algebra, equations, patterns and functions	Trigonometry, use of graphic calculators

In a workshop during the second year, the use of essential questions was formally introduced to all teachers. Even though some teachers were introduced to mapping for the first time, they were included in the essential questions, because enough teachers had been trained in mapping to help first-year teachers develop essential questions as they worked with their teams.

An emphasis was placed on standards by asking teachers to use state standards to develop skills. Although all standards cannot be covered during the year, teachers marked the standards they did teach. With student enrollment changing constantly, teachers could easily teach the same concept each month. However, marking standards kept teachers focused on what they had already taught and where they needed to go. This approach also raised teachers' awareness of all standards for their discipline.

Content Integration

At the beginning of the school year, a compilation of content areas was given to teachers and showed what had been taught the previous year. See Figure 8.5, which provides an example of content for four months during the previous year. This overview is from the elementary shelter program, which consists of grades 1–6. These documents were beginning points for discussion about what was to be taught in the current school year and how integration could occur.

As in the first year, a schedule similar to the one shown in Figure 8.2 was distributed to set time lines for maps to be submitted. This time line allowed teachers to be aware of when maps were due and kept them focused on thinking about coming events and lessons.

Although feedback continued, administrators found that it was not needed as intensely or as frequently as during the first year. With added training during the second year, it was evident that teachers were grasping the concept and excelling at the process of mapping. The following lists the time line for the second year of curriculum mapping:

•*Heidi Hayes Jacobs's one-day training.* The staff studies development of curriculum mapping.

•*Content integration.* Participants discuss how to align disciplines.

• *New technology.* A database is created so teachers can develop and share maps.

•*Essential question introduced.* Teachers are trained about the purposes of essential questions and how they should be written.

•*Self-assessment.* Teachers are asked how they feel about mapping.

Self-Evaluation

An anonymous survey was completed at the end of the second year, and the response was extremely positive. Teachers felt that essential questions helped them focus on the topics and that it became easier to develop essential questions as the year progressed. Teachers also felt that their mapping

Fig. 8.5 Compilation of Subject Content Entries: McKeesport Overview

	Science	Reading	Math	Language Arts	Social Studies	Physical Education
September	Summer Olympics: Australian mammals; water olympics: properties of water	Use the works of selected authors (Leo Lionni) to establish familiarity with the works and to generate comprehension and word recognition skills	Numbers: Expanded notation, place value, and reading numbers	Letter identification, sight words, grade-level word lists (spelling), reading comprehension	Themes: World geography, the history of the Olympic Games and of the stock market. Compare and contrast modern and ancient Olympics while incorporating map skills (scale systems); plus unit on Australia	Coordination and physical development activities are emphasized.
October	Spiders: structures, functions, unique characteristics; pumpkins: history, local farms	Use the works of selected authors (Eric Carle, R. L. Stevenson, William Armstrong, Jerry Spinelli) and the short story genre; explore story design through journal writings, plus plays and storyboards. Theme: "Spooky Stories"	Word problems: Vocabulary and symbols	Letter/word recognition, parts of speech, word study (prefixes and suffixes)	Themes: The election process and U.S. geography. Qualifications/powers/ roles of the president and vice president	Hand-to-eye coordination skills and gross motor skills. Pay attention skills and creative activities are emphasized

(continued)

Fig. 8.5   Compilation of Subject Content Entries: McKeesport Overview (cont.)

	Science	Reading	Math	Language Arts	Social Studies	Physical Education
November	Colors and changes in leaves, use of chromatography	Use the works of selected authors (Maurice Sendak, Judy Blume, Lois Lowry, Gary Paulsen) to become familiar with character analysis and interpretation of story plot. Theme: "Fall Harvest"	Measurement: Measuring using inches, estimation, and vocabulary	Letter/word recognition, sentence-paragraph writing	Theme: Fall harvest. Native Americans, pilgrims, and holidays; civics and government; the importance of rules in a society and how they are made; economics and how scarcity and choice influence decision making and behaviors	Cardiovascular skill improvement and more hand-to-eye coordination skills are emphasized
December	Asset kit: motion and design	Use the works of selected authors (Dr. Seuss, Chris Van Allsburg, Lois Lowry) to become familiar with summary writing, note-taking, and writing rubric. Theme: "Festival of Lights"	Measurement and Time: Measuring using meters, conversion, how to tell time, and how measurement and time relate	Letter and word recognition, rhyming, poetry	Theme: Festival of Lights. Develop knowledge of holidays and customs, countries of origin, research skills; civics and government; then compare types of government, student's rights vs. Bill of Rights	Continue cardiovascular activities and work on balance skills. Speed activities are emphasized

improved and that mapping had a purpose and was worthwhile. The following statements from teachers about this initiative were very encouraging:

• "Maps provided me with the opportunity to really think about ways to connect to the state standards and to use multiple teaching strategies."

• "My maps improved because of a focus on standards, skills, and assessments."

• "It was a good communication tool to use with other teachers."

Measuring Progress

A comparison of the curriculum maps that had been developed from the beginning of the first year to the end of the second year shows obvious improvement and growth.

The beginning maps listed verbs, such as *review, explain,* and *demonstrate,* as common tasks for developing skills. Later maps included verbs, such as *compare and contrast, predict, discover,* and *create,* as common processes for skill development. This shift in verbs shows evidence that teachers are requiring students to think at a higher level; consequently, their teaching reflects this requirement.

Although teachers were not required to include the standards in their maps for the first year, later maps show that teachers are now using the standards to develop skills. The standards are written in more detailed and defined terms rather than being treated as just an overall topic.

The resources listed on the maps include more Web sites and a richer selection of materials to supplement basic lesson resources, which clearly indicates that teachers are doing more research to find materials to supplement their lessons.

The beginning maps showed tests, quizzes, and observations as assessment methods. Later maps show that teachers are now including rubrics and performance assessments as part of their assessment methods.

The difference in the maps over the two years was astounding. There was obviously more reflection and focus on developing skills, standards, and assessments that were aligned to each other. Teachers' expectations for themselves and the students moved to a higher level. Teachers stated in the self-evaluation that they spent only one to two hours each month developing their maps and that those few hours dedicated to planning were worthwhile.

What's Next

With two years of mapping completed, there has been continuous improvement in the quality of the maps and the teachers' satisfaction with the process.

The third year will bring refinement of the maps with more consistent alignment of the standards, skills, and assessments. Training and feedback will continue to be invaluable strategies for helping teachers succeed with mapping. With the significant improvement in the curriculum design, how to teach to this curriculum plan will be the next major endeavor. Training about research-based instructional strategies will be part of future workshops during the upcoming school year. With the knowledge of instructional strategies, our teachers will excel at teaching students.

For our third year of mapping, we set the following goals:

• Refine maps for better alignment of standards, skills, and assessments.

• Be more specific as to the skills to be taught.

• Develop better instructional strategies that align to the skills.

As in the past two years, all staff members will have continuous training and feedback. As we look to the future, we realize that mapping ensures that all students who pass through our doors will experience a rich and varied curriculum—one that prepares them for *their* futures.

Creation of Benchmarks on the Building Map
Bilevel Analysis of Assessment Data

Heidi Hayes Jacobs

Benchmarks are used in many different settings, even in the natural environment. As we look at the student's journey through an array of tasks and goals, the way that a benchmark is used at an old inn in upstate New York might prove helpful. Hundreds of mountain trails weave through acres of deep forests on the inn's property in the Adirondacks. During construction of the inn in the early 1900s, the owners commissioned the building of a set of benchmarks at pivotal points along the winding trails. Each benchmark is an actual bench covered by a small protective roof. What is most striking is how the placement of those benchmark benches provides hikers a perfect view of where they have been, where they are, and where they are going.

In "edu-speak," the term *benchmark* has multiple meanings. Many terms in the field of education have different meanings for perfectly legitimate reasons. For the purposes of our discussion, a *benchmark goal* or *standard* is the common "bench" that all students should reach. A *benchmark task* is a common performance task or series of tasks using identical protocols that are given to groups of students for comparative purposes. This type of benchmark task can occur on an international, national, state, district, school, or classroom level.

For example, the International Baccalaureate program provides sets of tests and experiences that are standard for all participants worldwide. The SAT and SAT II tests, developed by the Educational Testing Service (ETS), and the advanced placement tests administered through the College Board are used as national sets of benchmark tasks on the secondary level. The purpose of those tests is to provide comparative data on students for a widely diffused market, such as a prospective college, or an employer, and for the individual student.

What is often missing in assessment and testing is a formal interim level of work at the school level. Because mapping provides the opportunity for a specific school to closely examine its students, it is possible to generate site-specific diagnosis and prescription. This chapter presents a curriculum mapping strategy for benchmark assessment tasks that are internally developed. The concept of bilevel analysis of assessment data is presented as a means of more refined work at the school level in response to student needs. The complex effects of state testing are considered, as well as the potential for using test data to benefit our learners. The response from staff development programs is suggested as part of the benchmark process. Laced throughout the chapter are examples of a middle school that used state testing data, bilevel analysis, and meaningful staff development processes to illustrate how mapping can bring relief to the real pressures that educators feel.

Anxiety Attacks Caused by State Benchmark Tests

State testing varies dramatically from state to state. Yet, every state test shares the same goal: accountability for districts, teachers, and students. A primary source of educational funding for public schools is state legislatures, which want to assure taxpayers that a system of accountability is in place. When one probes more deeply into the nature of state tests, it is interesting to note that widely discrepant information is revealed in those tests from state to state. New York has its famous Regents exams that require much more demanding levels of reading and writing in every subject area than tests given in many other states. Some states test only a few subjects. Most states test only certain grade levels, and the levels tested vary from state to state. Those discrepancies among the state benchmarks, the tests, and the grade levels tested make it impossible to compare students' scores across different states.

Today's fear about state tests is so great that it can drive curricular decisions in a way that is less than productive. Benchmark assessment tasks have generated an urgency that borders on panic. The results of comparative data often dramatically affect not only schools, districts, and state-takeover decisions, but also, and most directly, students. Some states give a school a rating, even a letter grade, as a ranking. Children hear about the acute anxiety surrounding those tests. Newspapers publish the scores as if testing were an intramural competition. Painfully, students know that in certain states and districts they might be held back a year on the basis of their test performance on one morning out of an entire school year. It is important to reflect on this notion, because—by virtue of limited time—the tests can assess only a handful of skills and a random selection of facts. Many concerned and caring educators work hard at state education departments trying to raise the level of teaching and learning. However, fair criticism can be raised about the actual level of proficiency revealed in a 60-minute, multiple-choice test given under duress in a room with thirty eight-year-olds.

Returning to the initial analogy of the benchmarks along the path presented in this chapter, we can see that the problem with most tests is that they really do not show where the hiker has been. They reveal a limited amount of information about where the learner is at the moment of the test, yet they are allowed to dictate where the child will be going. How can curriculum mapping help educators who are grappling with this anxious situation?

Use of Curriculum Mapping to Establish School Benchmarks

Rather than feeling ambushed by state education testing, a school can seize control of its responsibility to provide the right prescription for its learners. Ultimately, students attend specific schools in specific places and thus need specific remedies. Once a curriculum mapping database is in place, faculty members have an actual place to make cumulative and shared entries that address learner needs. The map serves as a public arena among professionals.

A natural outgrowth of curriculum mapping is the development of internally generated assessments of benchmarks that have been developed in an incremental pattern among teachers who share a target student population. The real power of benchmarking emerges when those benchmark tasks are placed on a map for ongoing formal review. Teachers can then share a common public commitment among the professional staff to carefully review ongoing progress or regression. It is the collective and collaborative nature of ongoing, shared examination of student work that promotes learner success. The key is that the group of teachers doing the examination is skillful at gap analysis and at the close scrutiny of what student work reveals. Curriculum mapping provides not only the calendar-based opportunity for such review, but also the shared language that can shortcut the process.

Instead of teaching to a test, teachers can work on skills that are needed on tests. Most likely, those skills are used in all kinds of situations, such as reading for meaning, responding in writing to problems, and organizing personal ideas clearly. Mapping focuses the collective efforts of staff members on the precise skills their school's students need to address. As William G. Ouchi (2003, pp. 141–42) points out:

A good school does make use of several different kinds of tests, but it's what it does with the test scores that makes the school successful. . . . It's like radar in an airplane—the pilot not only needs the information about where the stormy weather is, he or she has to use that information to alter the course. Finally, a good school has a consistent approach to children across teachers, subjects, and grade levels. Good data on students, a method of responding to the information, and consistency of response—these are the three elements of a sound focus on student achievement.

To illustrate how a school might employ these three elements, let us consider the case of Apple Valley Middle School, which is a composite of actual school sites. (The graphs in Figures 9.1–9.3 are from actual schools.)

Use of State Math Test Results to Revise Benchmarks: Apple Valley Middle School Responds

The scores on the 8th grade state math examinations at Apple Valley Middle School have arrived. The results are disappointing. The school had always had performance levels that seemed to reflect the basic bell curve, even with the increased transience of this Southern suburban town. The economic strata of the community cut across the working and middle class with increasing numbers of English as a Second Language (ESL) students. The district had pushed very hard. Therefore, the district thought that all students, including ESL, would do better on the math tests this year.

There were two fundamental types of test items: multiple choice and open response. Rubrics corresponded to four levels: mastery, proficient, basic, and below basic. All items certainly reflected reading acumen, given that every multiple-choice test required reading proficiency so students could answer questions correctly. Open response questions required reading and a written response. Before mapping, when scores had come back to the middle school, the reaction was to publish the scores in the local newspaper. The result was teachers and students were pummeled, both in letters to the editor and in angry declarations at school board meetings. Obviously, publishing and pummeling did not work, because the scores were still disappointing.

Now Apple Valley Middle School has curriculum mapping as an alternative way to work on improving student performance. Faculty members have a more effective way of learning from the tests, translating those findings into instructional actions, and planning for those revisions as a community of teachers. All teachers know that there is no such thing as an 8th grade test. The state test is, in fact, a cumulative test—a grade 8-7-6-5-4-3-2-1-K test. Rather than spinning individual wheels while trying to cram every math proficiency into the one year that a teacher has the student, Apple Valley's teachers are looking at the big picture. Their plan is to carefully analyze testing data from the state in conjunction with what they have learned in their own classroom assessments. As Marzano (2000, p. 87) points out, "A few well-planned and well-formatted assessments provide far better information about student achievement than do multiple assessments poorly planned and formatted." Teachers will view the findings of state and classroom assessments together and will diagnose together as a team. They will make appropriate cumulative revisions together.

The graph in Figure 9.1 simply shows the overall scores. Analyzing this table cannot help the teachers much.

The graph in Figure 9.2 cannot help teachers either. The scores are reported by type—multiple choice and open response—but these data are still too broad to be of any help. Even breaking data down by math section is of little value.

What those teachers know they need are the original tests and the item analysis as shown in Figure 9.3. That benchmark contends that steady and credible results can emerge in a targeted group of learners when a new approach is used.

Bilevel Item Analysis

A school can establish meaningful benchmark assessments through the mapping process by using what I identify as a bilevel analysis process. That process helps a school's faculty use assessment data to do the following:

• Identify needed skills and concepts that are subject specific.

• Identify needed literacy strategies that are required to carry out the task.

• Establish benchmark tasks on both levels.

• Enter those tasks on maps.

• Review the results.

• Monitor each student's growth.

When we attempt to learn from student performance data, we are not simply doing an item analysis. Rather, the process involves taking apart data on the following two distinctive tiers from various types of assessments: state testing, classroom portfolios, and classroom tasks:

• *Tier one is an analysis of the concept and content that relate directly to the subject matter itself.* If a math test is on percents, then, obviously, teachers need to figure out to what extent students are struggling with the concept of percentages. Teachers might explore alternative approaches to helping students, such as using manipulatives, analogies, or technology; they must see if there are basic computation skills lacking.

• *Tier two—an analysis of the requisite language capacity necessary to carry out the task— is the very root of all student performance.* Language capacity is often overlooked. If students cannot read the test items, then they cannot carry out the tasks. Certainly, it is possible—if not common—for students to demonstrate a basic math concept in class. However, when students encounter the same concept presented in text form, they may struggle. Weak interaction with text often frustrates students. Students read the words, but they do not have meaning for them. Therefore, we need to analyze both tiers if we are to determine a sustained prescriptive approach that will enable learners to achieve success.

Langer, Colton, and Goff (2003, p. 71) underscore that documentation is of critical importance to the collaborative analysis of student work. Teachers at Apple Valley are doing an item-by-item analysis of students' test results. Let's return to our case study to find out what their analysis revealed.

Results of Bilevel Analysis by Apple Valley

The teachers found that, indeed, some concepts were problematic in certain strands on both the multiple choice and open response questions. For example, students in grade 8 clearly struggled with pre-algebra. Rather

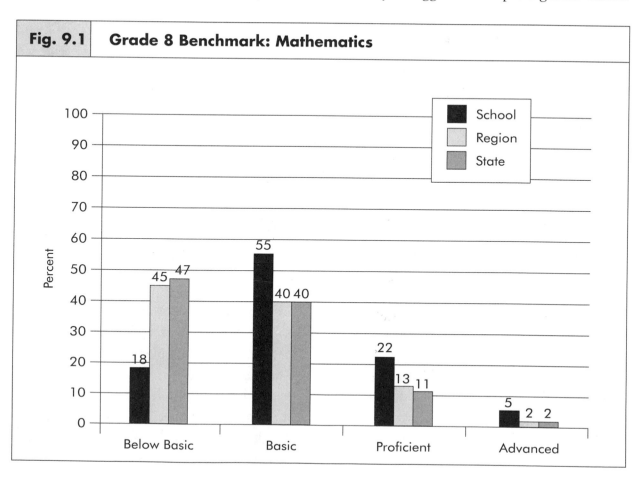

Fig. 9.1   Grade 8 Benchmark: Mathematics

than just analyzing the math issues, the teachers went deeper to analyze the second tier—the linguistic tier. Using item analysis (as in Figure 9.3), they found some patterns of significance to the learners. The teachers noticed that on open response items that were composed of word problems in paragraphs, students missed items with significantly greater frequency if paragraphs had more than four sentences. Teachers looked carefully at the high-frequency words, which are the words used as protocols to determine the nature of the action to be taken. As directives, those words are signposts to actions. Therefore, students who misread or misunderstand such words are going off in the wrong direction.

Action Steps Using Mapping

Teachers compiled the high-frequency words and found that many of them, such as *reason, determine, identify, compare, contrast, evaluate,* and *detail,* kept appearing on the list. To determine whether those words were truly problematic, the teachers simply listed the words and asked their students to define each one in their own words. The teachers were stunned to find out how limited the students were in accomplishing this basic task. In part, the limitation seems logical, because students rarely use such words in their natural speech. These were testing words, or assignment words. The teachers also circled and gathered the words that indicated specialized math terminology; they recognized that those words were key to understanding the actual math premise and computational forms requested on the test items. Examples of specialized terms are *denominator, ratio, parabola,* and *fraction.*

At this point, it would have been natural for the teachers to retreat to their classrooms and hammer away at the concepts and the words. But because this school used curriculum mapping, the teachers were able to implement a 21st-century solution. They worked effectively as a team by using their maps as the basis for sustained joint revision. The teachers collaboratively developed a series of benchmark tasks that built incrementally through the grades and that focused on the precise skills needing attention.

There were two formal entries on the maps for site-based benchmarks. Those items were developed as a string of spiraling tasks focusing on the root issues that hindered student performance at the school. Teachers worked with the three elementary schools that fed students to them, and they formally entered tasks. Twice each year, on the maps for November and March, there was a designated week when all math teachers in grades K–8 assessed the student's ability to read multistep word problems. Everyone knew what each grade was working on and that those tasks would require deliberate and effective instructional attention leading up to the designated benchmark week. After the designated benchmark week, assessment data

Fig. 9.2	8th Grade Benchmark: Mathematics Strands

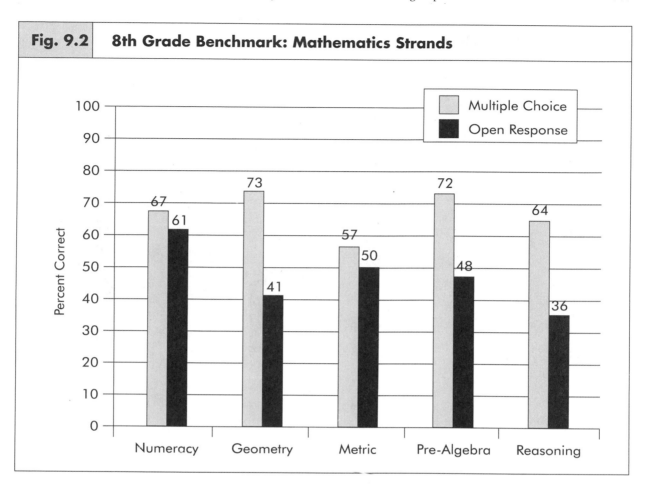

The faculty members sorted specialized vocabulary terms according to their appropriateness at specific grade levels. The key was to be active in assessing vocabulary deployment. Simply looking up a term was insufficient. Each month, sets of words were posted for students to use in all their writing and in their speech. The students knew that those were the words needing attention, and they approached the task with what can be

were available on every student concerning the specific math concepts and the language and reading strategies that require attention.

described only as relief. Often in text and in a teacher's speech, words are used with an assumption that the learners know them well—a false assumption. Some of the most glaring errors occur on state tests because students give the wrong meaning to the words. It is tough for 13-year-olds to admit that they are unclear about the meaning of the words *contrast, determine,* or *infer.* Often students simply hobble along through important testing days feeling a real anxiety about where they are going and where their test results will send them in the future.

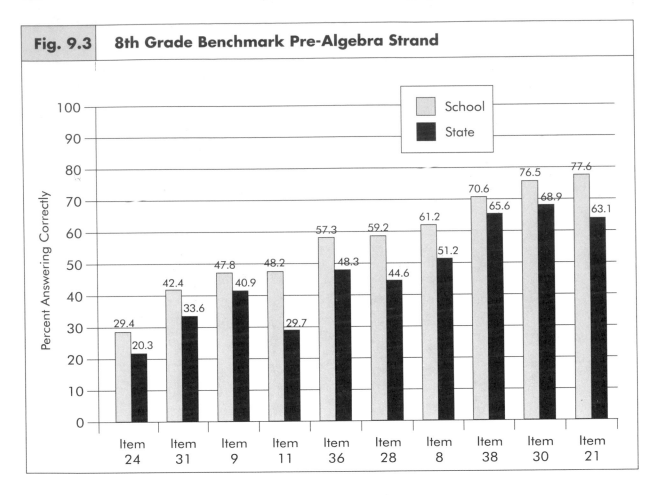

Fig. 9.3 | **8th Grade Benchmark Pre-Algebra Strand**

Establishment of a Benchmark Week on the Map

With a date posted on the curriculum map, teachers can begin to work toward a designated benchmark week in their schools. Every classroom is involved on targeted skills and vocabulary appropriate for each grade level or team. Students know the targeted skills as well, but with a very different sensibility. Johnny can honestly say, "This is not the phantom SATs or the state test out to get me. This is the week that the teachers in my school are going to be focused on the things I need to be working on."

All staff development in the school is aimed toward helping teachers make instructional adjustments that correspond to the necessary targets. Staff development should be about what the students need teachers to be developing at the site level. Therefore, if there are problems with writing in response to math problems, workshops in that area might be warranted. The past has seen a tendency toward having inservice training that is based on filling credit. As a profession, teachers should take a second look at the way we match our staff development hours with the specific issues that occur at the site level.

During the benchmark week, all students are engaged in the identified benchmark tasks. If the tasks are well crafted, the skills being addressed will merge naturally with the ongoing content. For example, if students are struggling with multistep word problems in math and if during the benchmark week the math teacher is engaged in a unit on percent, the multistep word problems will deal with percent problems.

At the end of the week, there is a remarkable new body of data. Assessments from all students are available cumulatively. In the K–5 elementary school that sends its students to the middle school, there are now responses to multistep word problems. The 4th grade developed an essential map in concert with the 8th grade benchmark week (see Figure 9.4). The smart principal will build in review time frames during the subsequent week for groups of teachers to view the progress of all learners. Common sense tells us that if we target a set of needed skills and refocus our instruction on those skills, if we develop corresponding teaching strategies in a collaborative group to assist students on those skills, and if we formally reassess students' progress, we will likely see improvement. The Ohio State Education Department published the results of a study carried out by Indiana University's Center for Evaluation

(Kercheval & Newbill 2001). The study identified those practices used by selected schools to increase student achievement and documented those practices in sufficient detail so that other districts could use those examples. The most frequently cited strategies—listed in order—were these:

- Curriculum alignment and mapping
- Professional development focused on areas of need specific to the schools
- A focus on literacy
- Ongoing analysis and tracking of performance data
- Intervention and remediation
- Test preparation strategies

Continuous review, adjustment, and growth are the bottom line in teaching and learning.

Review of Internally Generated Data

Teachers feel a genuine sense of professionalism as they sit around a table and look at the student work produced during the benchmark week. In particular, this sense can be true if they agree on the terms for diagnosis. Rubrics can be most helpful as educators attempt to judge the quality of work produced by learners. When a common set of criteria is used, there is a common language of descriptors. A match between the precise skills entered on the map and the precise language used on the rubric is crucial for the review of internally mapped benchmarks.

Fig. 9.4　Essential Curriculum for 8th Grade Algebra

	February	March	April	May
Essential Questions	• Why study algebra? • Why collect and plot data? • When would you use compound interest in real life?	• Why study algebra? • How do you find the value of unknowns? • How do you use math in your life?	• Why study algebra? • When would you use systems of equations and inequalities in real-life situations?	• Why study algebra? • Why is problem solving important?
Content	Slopes and lines, exponents, and powers *Terms:* slope	Application to real-world problems *Terms:* theorem, exponential	Polynomials and linear systems *Terms:* polynomial, linear, proportion	Factoring and review of algebra
Skills	• Simplifies expression involving exponents • Simplifies powers of positives and negatives • Collects and plots data; writes an equation for and uses a line of best fit • Writes an equation in standard form given a real-life situation	• Identifies cells, rows, and columns in spreadsheet • Writes algebraic equations to represent constant increase/decrease situations • Uses proportions to find missing sides of similar figures	• Multiplies polynomials • Adds and subtracts polynomials • Factors out a greatest common factor from a polynomial • Factors trinomials and difference of squares	• Factors binomials • Uses the greatest common factor • Factors using easy and difficult FOIL • Uses special factors to factor; "2-Rule Drop" out • Solves problems using factoring

(continued)

Fig. 9.4 Essential Curriculum for 8th Grade Algebra (cont.)

Skills	• Converts back and forth from standard form and slope-intercept form • Graphs linear inequalities from situations • Evaluates powers of real numbers • Calculates compound interest • Solves and graphs problems involving exponential growth and decay • Uses the properties of exponents	• Applies and solves Pythagorean Theorem • Finds area of rectangular figures • Calculates compound interest • Calculates and represents graphically exponential growth and decay • Solves percent problems • Writes formula for a cell in a spreadsheet	• Classifies polynomials by degree and number of terms • Performs all operations on polynomials • Uses polynomials in real-life situations • Solves system of two linear equations • Solves any linear equation in one variable • Solves any inequality in one variable • Solves proportions composed of linear expressions	• Reviews solving equations • Reviews problem solving
Assessments	• Daily assignments • Notebook • Stroop Test • Short answer and free response quiz and test	• End-of-unit test on solving equations • T-Shirt Dilemma Performance Task • Journal entry on real-world problem solving • Original math problem for 5th grade • Math game using criteria on scoring rubric • *Benchmark:* Multi-step work problem on practical application	• Daily assignments • Notebook • Short answer and free response • Quiz and test	• Daily assignments • Notebook • Short answer and free response quiz and test

For example, if students are working on writing responses that use clear and logical language in response to math word problems, then the rubric should have criteria for precise and logical language. The purpose of a rubric is to provide the learner with a public and clarifying set of reminders about not only what quality work looks like, but also what the target and purpose of the benchmark week will be. Sometimes students simply feel they are being tested for a grade as opposed to having a learning opportunity.

The match is made between the rubric and the skills addressed and assessed on the map. Alignment is much more than linking with state standards. Alignment means designing a direct line between what our assessment data reveals and how our curriculum should be revised to address the needs of students cumulatively. Alignment is a direct line from class to class as we follow the student's journey through a school. With its immediate accessibility through technology, curriculum mapping provides a forum for designating actions to be taken between the team of teachers who share the learners. Anchoring the review process in benchmarks on the maps provides clear points of reference for all professionals in a school.

Staff Development That Is Based on Results of Benchmarks

Staff development should shift to match the focus on school-based, internally generated benchmarks. Too often, professional development requirements (sometimes called professional improvement plans) amount to a requirement for random inservice credit. Teachers and administrators look at a menu of course offerings. The courses themselves may have value, and they may provide stimulating experiences. The question, however, should be, "Are these courses needed for students in our school?"

Instead of requiring teachers to "take something" to fulfill a requirement, we should be developing what the learners in our schools need us to develop. The link should be clear between unpacked assessment data and what is planned for professional development. When Apple Valley found that students were struggling with reading and writing strategies in math, workshops and staff development were directed toward assisting teachers in this area. Clearly, the reading and writing strategies were concerns that went beyond the math department. Apple Valley faculty members, as a group, took on a more consistent and thorough approach to reading and writing strategies. They could see that the deficiencies that came up on the math benchmarks were core problems in other benchmarked experiences. When they examined the collection of essays at a benchmark portfolio check, the social studies and English departments found that students needed help with editing written work for more consistency. In short, the decision was to dedicate all staff development toward the desired result of improving students' reading and writing strategies.

Ways to Link Teacher Growth to Student Growth

We can know that our efforts for professional development are successful when we see targeted gains in student performance. When there is a systemic focus with a common place to share findings, the conditions for success grow. Mapping becomes that arena. Curriculum mapping becomes a kind of electronic town square where teachers in a school have access to each other's work and can make cumulative and powerful decisions over time.

An exciting option that fuses curriculum mapping technology and staff development is the professional development training that hyperlinks online to the maps. For example, if a new teacher needs assistance with learning to design units of study, a principal or supervisor can link that teacher to an online course designed by Public Broadcasting System's *PBS TeacherLine* (see Curriculum Mapping Resources, p. 170) or a local regional service center. In this way, the map becomes the instructional hub for both students and teachers. Corresponding online coursework can respond directly to the assessment benchmarks placed on the map by teachers.

Working with a school that possesses a paper database in files and that makes professional development decisions on the basis of fulfilling a point requirement is an oddly dated experience. In contrast, working with a school that has been involved with electronic mapping for several years and that has an active database that it uses to make professional decisions is a strikingly contemporary experience. A sense of renewal and possibility is based on evidence. Teachers and administrators have come up for air and can work as a genuine team. In its way, the school has reached its own benchmark. The school team can see where it has been, where it is now, and where it should go to help learners prepare for their futures.

Curriculum Mapping as a Hub

Integrating New Forms of Data, Decision-Making Structures, and Staff Development

Heidi Hayes Jacobs

We go to too many meetings in education. We educators have so much to accomplish and so many pressures that it is understandable why school leaders perpetually organize groups and subgroups of people to solve the problems. A school district might have an assessment committee, a scheduling committee, a standards committee, a philosophy committee, and myriad curriculum committees. The groups meet separately, although clearly each group's mission depends on all the other areas. The illusion is that somehow final decisions will seamlessly link with the findings from the committees. One contributing factor to this disarray is the lack of a centralized hub for information and data. The diffusion model creates confusion. Curriculum mapping can become a hub to focus the most critical efforts and to shed those that are extraneous to student progress. The electronic nature of communication changes both the time and the space needed for meetings. We can meet flexibly using the Internet.

Curriculum maps have the potential to become the hub for making decisions about teaching and learning. Focusing the barrage of initiatives and demands on schools into a central database that can be accessed from anywhere through the Internet can provide relief. Schools can have a common electronic town square to bring all the players together. By fusing assessment data with mapping data, we are producing new types of knowledge to give us new types of instructional solutions. Mapping becomes an integrating force to address not only curriculum issues, but also programmatic ones. It is easy to ask a district, "What initiatives from your state or school could be integrated and handled directly through mapping?" Responses often include No Child Left Behind legislation, alignment with standards, literacy programs, and new math programs. Mapping gives a team of educators a central forum and a place to reach into each classroom. At the same time, the team can step back and see the wide-angle view about dealing with new demands.

In this chapter, I will identify key causes for fragmentation in our institutions and will make a case for the "hub effect." I will suggest ways to rethink decision-making structures, integrate data, and create powerful staff development responses. The center of the wheel is a grounding force that holds the spokes together and allows for forward movement. The continual complaints about too many initiatives, too little time, and too much waste for too few results will drain a school's energy. With commitment and imagination, mapping can become a liberating solution to some of those perpetual problems.

Some Causes for Fragmented Decision Making?

Extreme tendencies emerge in the way districts and schools handle information under the duress of helping students perform. In workshops, I have often asked participants to draw a flowchart that shows the participant's perception of the current way that curriculum decisions are actually being made and how they reach students. The directions are these: "Note the external and internal forces and groups that affect classroom curriculum decisions. Be sure to include how (and if) assessment data affect the curriculum's decision-making process." It is fascinating to see the wide range of responses that emerge from a group of educators who are from the same location when they respond to that protocol.

Obviously, curriculum comes from somewhere, whether it is dictated by a state education department or constructed by learners. Following the flow of decision making in educational settings reveals the inadequacies of our current decision-making schemes. One extreme is that decisions are made in the isolation of the teacher's classroom. Feeling pummeled by the outside pounding of tests and standards, a teacher can easily hide and simply turn to the immediacy of the classroom. It is not surprising that many teachers burrow in their rooms with all that they know about their students. There is no place to take the information.

The other extreme is district overdrive, oversight, and Orwellian control. A conforming mentality toward standardization hides the real agenda of fear. We are afraid that we cannot meet the needs of the learners, so at least we will control everything that we can. The tendency toward a cookie-cutter, one-size-fits-all approach is also understandable.

District leadership feels just as pummeled by the outside pressure of tests and standards, and local taxpayers are at the gates. The reaction to state, national, and local assessment data is often to form another committee or, in a broad fashion, to throw a workshop at the general areas of concern for teachers. If we step back, it is clear that the intentions are worthy, but they are not formally connected with the ongoing daily experience of students actually receiving instruction over the years. A meticulous point–counterpoint diagnosis and a prescription linking assessment data and the curriculum are a rarity.

We need a decision-making alternative, because students are the victims of those extreme tendencies. Curriculum mapping shifts the flow of information and the means of presenting the information. It allows for the elimination of extraneous and needless committees. It provides a focal point at the site for all who are concerned with a specific group of learners. Because mapping programs house all tiers of data needed in a school, mapping does, indeed, become an integrating hub. The integration model creates clarity. It does not eliminate conflict in decision making, but rather it focuses conflict into productive discussion and debate. Perhaps one of the reasons for anger and frustration in our schools centers around people who are working very hard but in isolation. With a new level of integrated and dynamic data, schools can begin to plan and to create schedules and structures that support cumulative decision-making patterns.

Hub for a 21st Century School: Cumulative Decision Making

With mapping data being electronic, fluid, and accessible to everyone through the Internet, a new kind of decision-making structure is not only possible but also crucial. But if mapping is superimposed on an old decision-making structure, there is a culture clash. It is a clash between a 21st-century data format and a 19th-century committee structure. What is needed is a forward-looking structure that is based on the actual pattern and flow of the student population.

In *Mapping the Big Picture: Integrating Curriculum and Assessment K–12* (Jacobs, 1997a), the chapter titled "A Case for the Elimination of Curriculum Committees" seemed a logical outgrowth of the mapping process. Now, after years of working with schools on mapping, it is clear that we need to refocus school decision-making structures so I can enable schools to design for the future. When schools move toward developing site-based teaching and learning councils, they can effectively use a new form of data through a curriculum map. With a more streamlined form for deliberation and a more dynamic database to consider, schools are poised to deliver a higher level of instruction. In fact, when old-style curriculum committees and diffused decision patterns from the past attempt to use contemporary data through maps, there can be paralysis. Maps can become interesting forms of information that have no place to go. Mapping can become "one more thing we have to deal with in our district." The reverse is also true. If an effective decision-making structure uses old forms of data, then the resulting decisions are more likely to be flawed because the source information is not accurate. In short, form and function need to match.

Curriculum mapping can provide the hub for effective decision making as teachers enter ongoing data, review those data with other teachers who share their students, and take apart assessment data to find clues to what students need. Stepping back from our traditional, or in some instances antiquated, scheduling formats is a natural outgrowth of mapping. Practical questions emerge, such as who should be meeting with whom.

In a nutshell, often the wrong people are meeting together with the wrong information and are often inadvertently creating the very gaps they wish to eliminate in a child's journey through school. The following guiding questions can help organize a school that is armed with an active electronic database:

• Who should be meeting with whom to maximize student learning?

• What existing committees could be eliminated?

• How might our schedule be rethought to support communication between the right people?

• When can electronic meetings effectively replace appointment-based committee work?

We need to structure the school setting to promote focused teaching and learning. When a school or district has worked for several years in the mapping process, a natural need emerges to streamline the three primary structures of a school to support better communication. The following three key programmatic structures house curriculum and instruction:

• Schedule (daily, annual, long-term)

• Grouping of students (within classrooms, throughout the institution, and by class size)

• Grouping of personnel (into teams, departments, and roles)

The decisions made about how those structures are shaped have a direct effect on curriculum, assessment, and instruction. The habituated routine of working within burdensome structures shackles efforts to grow an enriched curriculum.

Let us return to the question of, "Who is meeting with whom?" What becomes clear is that we are not necessarily meeting with the right people to enhance learning. It becomes equally clear that decisions about the structure of the schedule make optimum meeting times prohibitive. When I visit elementary schools across the country, it is clear that most schools have schedules orchestrated to enable grade-level teachers to meet together. Those meetings are the most frequent, common, and exclusive focus of planning in elementary schools. The 3rd grade teachers meet together regularly, if not daily. This fact is disturbing when considering the potential effect on Johnny. Why have people meeting regularly, if not daily, who do not share the same group of students? A student moves from kindergarten to 1st to 2nd to 3rd grade, not across 3rd grade. It is understandable that 3rd grade teachers can benefit from periodic shared experiences, but careful planning rarely occurs on an ongoing basis along the actual path the student follows. I am not saying that this is an either/or situation, but currently it is extreme in most of our schools.

Consider high school. The rarest meeting is for all teachers who teach the same students in the ninth grade to sit together and actually examine their students' work. However, the actual pattern involving freshman students is to progress from teacher to teacher. The schedule is designed to ensure that department meetings occur all the time. Again, as in the elementary example, there is a purpose for meeting periodically in a department, but students actually need much greater communication between the chain of care among the teachers who are responsible for their days in school. In short, the wrong people meet too often and with the wrong information.

When one works in a business, the usual protocol is to identify a problem and to determine the best grouping of people to solve the problem. Education is a business—the growth business. It cultivates the growth of our learners, translates the growth of new knowledge, and builds professional growth.

Vertical Planning Teams at the Elementary Level

Who should meet together? When one considers the needs of students at different stages during their journey through school, ongoing vertical meetings in elementary schools make good sense. In the precious early years of schooling, students need to have their preK–2 teachers meeting and sharing regularly. Currently, they do not meet. An *event mentality* is when teachers meet twice a year on a professional day. On those days, the one group of teachers who really could make a big difference in helping students learn to read spend two hours in a "breakout" meeting after a keynote session in the auditorium. Students who are showing early signs of struggle in developing language capacity can be red-flagged by the vertical group. Performance data, coupled with teacher observation material, can serve to inform curriculum adjustments on the map in a cumulative decision-making pattern.

These are the key years—the most important years—for building literacy, and yet most of our schools are not organized to provide regular, ongoing review of student progress among the team that is most likely to make these key years productive. With mapping data, the review teams have immediate access to ongoing documentation. When a grade-level meeting is warranted or scheduled, the same maps will assist the value of periodic sharing among grade-level teachers in terms of developing strategies to more effectively do their jobs.

Cross-Disciplinary Review Teams in High Schools

Just as it is desirable for elementary teachers to meet regularly in a vertical pattern to help monitor student progress over time and across grades, it is also true for high school teachers to meet frequently in a horizontal pattern across subjects. In a high school students have a group of teachers each day; they do not attend a department. As stated, the rarest of meetings, for example, is for all people who teach 9th grade to be in one room together, although school is Johnny's experience.

Nonetheless, departments do have a prominent and crucial role in planning and preparing curriculum work, but they need to clarify what that role is and what it is not. If a physics teacher is concerned about performance but meets on a regular basis only with the science department, then an obvious gap develops. A key variable when determining reasoning in physics is the student's mathematical conceptual understanding of equations. With mapping, teachers in math and science can have immediate electronic access to a warehouse of data about the vertical route from middle school into high school in both the sciences and mathematics. With many on the high school staff concerned about reading and writing strategies,

working in departmental fortresses will be insufficient as a solution. Site-based work on the curriculum council provides an opportunity to make alterations on maps across a grade level. Again, cumulative decision-making patterns should sustain and follow the actual path of the learner through school.

A Medical Meeting Analogy

There is a natural medical analogy when discussing curriculum mapping and meetings. If a patient is admitted to the hospital for surgery, who among the professionals should meet to give the best possible care? Who should meet to work toward ultimate recovery and health? The best interest of the patient is served when the surgeon works with the chain of care—from the internal medicine physician, to the receiving nurse, to the anesthesiologist, to the pulmonary specialist, to the nutritionist.

In short, decisions must be made among the actual people who are going to attend to the patient's needs. Certainly surgeons require and depend on professional dialogue with their surgeon peer group. Yet, no hospital would schedule most of its time for those meetings at the expense of having the people meet who share the same patients. One place where there is no opportunity for thoughtful planning and preparation is the emergency room, where medical personnel know almost nothing about the prior record or experience of each arriving patient. There is an urgent, anxious tone to the set of decisions that must be made quickly without benefit of a strong understanding of the patient's experience. Sometimes it seems as if we give an emergency room education, because we have so little good information about our learners.

We should not accede the decision-making authority to habitual formats such as grade level or department groupings. Neither should we send it to a distant galaxy of committees far from the child in the classroom. Nor should we encourage the micromanagement isolationism of one teacher out of the many whom each student will deal with. Our clear and sensible alternative is to vest the greatest authority to the collection of teachers at the site who can actually make a difference when acting collectively. Site-based teaching and learning councils coupled with an active electronic database of curriculum maps and assessment data can replace our old way of working and can become the decision-making hub.

Targeted Work Groups Versus Eternal Committees

Task forces with targeted projects can be organized flexibly to respond to specific emerging needs. When the work of a task force is completed, it is disbanded. Task forces are different from the rigidly formed committees that often have little contact with one another. When specific concerns emerge from a mapping review, a study group can be formed to examine problems. It works at the behest of the site-based council or the district cabinet. Building councils and district cabinets establish a task force to become a targeted work group to pursue pertinent research and to develop solutions. The task force members should include a collection of people who will be best suited to address problems. Sometimes this grouping means people who are not in the same department.

In short, educators should go only to those meetings that they need to attend and should have the best data available. We should not go to meetings of committees out of habit. A flexible and goal-oriented group is possible through the electronic accessibility of a curriculum map. In the past, it was not easy to establish problem-responsive working groups, because there was no immediate access to centralized data. Technology is challenging us to rethink not only paper and pencil outcomes, but also the very way we organize to wrestle with organizational formats and systems.

Time Lines for Developing Site-Based Teaching and Learning

The commitment to curriculum mapping is labor intensive during the start-up year. Curriculum mapping can be a demanding process as a school shifts to a new form of documenting and reviewing practices. Thus, I would suggest that moving to site-based curriculum councils will evolve during the second year of mapping. Overloading the system burns fuses. However, during the first year, the planning team is wise to begin looking ahead to prepare for a more efficient decision-making structure. The planning team can begin by asking and gathering information in response to the following questions:

• Who currently meets with whom and for what purpose?

• What are the actual teacher patterns our students follow over the day and over the years?

• What number of teachers might constitute a representative site council?

• How often should we meet to help our learners?

• What types of in-person meetings that we now have could be replaced with electronic meetings?

• What might the job description be for the council?

• Should the council positions rotate?

• What committees can we shed?

• What task forces or study teams might be good to begin assisting the council?

The natural outgrowth of this self-examination is that schools will rethink the time, content, and direction of staff development. Not only can the hub effect create more integrated decision-making functions, but also it can, in turn, create more sophisticated, nuanced, and productive staff development.

A Hub for Designing Differentiated Staff Development

Step back and look at the range of people in any given faculty, and you will see a range of professional needs and possibilities. Cookie-cutter instruction for students doesn't work for professionals either. Too many states and districts require a certain number of in-service credits for "just-show-up-and-prove-you-have-a-pulse" experiences. The time, money, and effort that are poured into staff development need an upgrade too. Curriculum mapping in conjunction with site-based teaching and learning councils gives schools a chance to move to a dynamic type of staff development.

We should be developing our staff on the basis of what the students in the school need the staff to develop. As noted in Chapter 9 of this book, our analysis of assessment data should give the site-based council a clear direction for professional development. Teacher growth should clearly correspond to student growth. Staff development should be matched to demonstrable gains in student performance. Individual teacher needs vary within schools, and staff development can and should focus on what individual teachers need so they can address the precise student performance gaps in a school.

Instead of pro forma staff development, where each teacher takes arbitrary credits through a college or in-service program, professional development should be targeted precisely toward what the teachers need in their schools (See appendixes 8 and 9 for examples of targeted staff development plans). This philosophy means that different teachers are likely to be functioning at different levels of expertise. Obviously, if a group of teachers needs technology skills to enable the group to map, then staff development should help the group do so. If a group of teachers has had limited experience in writing curriculum, then staff development can help that group. If there is a need for learning about item analysis of testing data, then the teachers who need this work should be participating. We should think imaginatively about venues for professional development.

Online courses can appear right on a map that might assist teachers in their work. For example, a science department chair might direct a group of teachers to a PBS Concept to Classroom course on WebQuests to update and improve the quality of the group's investigative work. The hyperlink could appear right on the teachers' maps (see Curriculum Mapping Resources, pp. 170–171).

One-size-fits-all staff development may cause faculty defections. Teachers have different backgrounds and competencies for different purposes, yet sometimes our professional development is too uniform. Adult professionals resent attending workshops that do not match their needs. Adult professionals also recognize that there are always new practices and new knowledge to learn. Consider an example when a school elects to take on

curriculum mapping. Following the prologue planning stage, the planners and faculty members are ready to enter data into their maps. Two distinctive skills are requisite for successful data entry: proficiency and experience with writing and designing curriculum, and ease and competence with computer usage. If we look at Figure 10.1 and use a quadrant model for the two aforementioned skills, the school leadership can start to get a handle on how to set up appropriately targeted strategies for staff development.

Note that teachers in Quadrant 1 have high competence in curriculum writing but are novices at the computer. Does it not make good sense that they could use computer lab time to get help in transferring their curriculum work to the computer? This approach would be in contrast to those teachers in Quadrant 2 who are capable of "taking off" with mapping by virtue of their curriculum experience and computer know-how. A straightforward demonstration of data entry will likely suffice. Those teachers in Quadrant 3 are likely to be individuals who are new to teaching but are very comfortable with technology. There is even the possibility of pairing these teachers with those in Quadrant 1. The final group probably is struggling on many fronts and will need particular care and attention from staff developers.

In short, staff development grouping and strategies should support the needs of the professionals in a school. Whether training comes through a workshop, an online

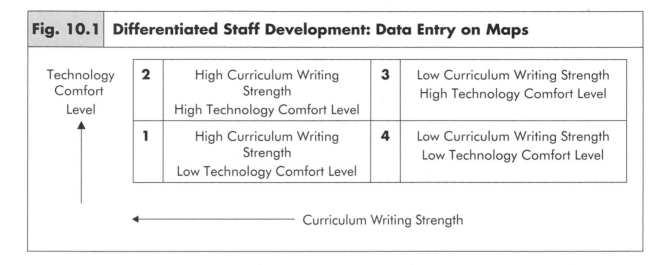

Fig. 10.1 | Differentiated Staff Development: Data Entry on Maps

Technology Comfort Level	2	High Curriculum Writing Strength High Technology Comfort Level	3	Low Curriculum Writing Strength High Technology Comfort Level
	1	High Curriculum Writing Strength Low Technology Comfort Level	4	Low Curriculum Writing Strength Low Technology Comfort Level

Curriculum Writing Strength

course, a videoconference, a site visit, a study group, a conference, a peer coaching session, or a mentor, mapping can serve as a common reference point for participants. For example, Susan Udelhofen and Kathy Larson (2002) have made a tremendous contribution in their writing by linking curriculum mapping to the mentoring process. They have helped us structure experiences for new teachers during the mentoring year, and they advocate the use of curriculum maps to foster communication between the new teacher and the mentor. Some schools are even mapping the mapping process, as well as mapping professional development plans. Many new teachers use projected maps as a planning tool with mentors, as do preservice teachers in their coursework at universities.

When schools take on exciting professional development programs, such as Understanding by Design (UBD; Wiggins & McTighe, 1998), Dimensions of Learning (Marzano, 1992), Concept-Based Curriculum (Erickson, 1998), or Differentiated Instruction (Tomlinson, 1999), mapping not only provides, but also beckons, the integration of those programs into the maps. The actual templates of maps suggest the inclusion of those instructional features. For example, lesson and unit templates in UBD can be plugged into the lesson planner section of the map. Key concepts at the basis of curriculum planning would be entered in the content and essential question entry points. With Differentiated Instruction, we click on the map and place a tab that says "differentiated instruction" and "go deeper" into our lesson plans as we document the grouping of learners and the corresponding instructional adjustments that have been made. In this way the map is a literal hub for initiatives.

In their timely book on transforming school culture, Zmuda, Kuklis, and Kline (2004) detail the power of forging connections between UBD and curriculum mapping to promote a "more complex, richer conception or curriculum":

> When school staff have a more informed conception of curriculum, a teacher's daily decisions about how to deliver instruction not only affect student achievement in that classroom but also future student achievement, for it is assumed that students will be entering the next classroom prepared to handle a more sophisticated or more expansive level of work. (p. 122)

A Hub for Planning Future Directions with New Data

Speed is not the only advantage that technology provides to educational decision making. Merging data sources will help us create new knowledge, as Kallick and Wilson tell us in Chapter 7 of this book. This new knowledge can give us new solutions, and we will need corresponding new directions for staff development. In the future, curriculum mapping and its electronic format can lead us toward including a focus on student curriculum maps, where learners can document their own progress and can communicate that progress to teachers. Homework from the teacher's map to the student's map seems a logical outgrowth. With the increase in bandwidth and the access to a wide array of media, it is easy to envision assignments given in direct reference to documentary footage or videoconferencing and netcam interviews. Parents can be involved with direct communication as they relate to the map that assists in describing the path the student is on during the school year. There will be more access to technology, not less, in the future, and the access itself will be easier, more reliable, and more imaginative.

Unquestionably, the future will bring wireless and compact hardware, which will promote easy access to maps from any location. In the near future, the map will be a traveling hub. We will be able to communicate not only with colleagues in our schools and districts, but also with colleagues across learning communities. Web site resources exist today that link teachers all over the world. Those links will continue to proliferate.

A vivid moment occurred during a trip when I was changing flights at O'Hare International Airport in Chicago. As I was walking to my gate, I saw a familiar-looking gentleman typing furiously away on his laptop as he waited for a flight. He looked up and smiled. He was a high school social studies teacher from a district in which I had worked in the past. He said, "Hey, look at this. Here I am at O'Hare mapping away!" It is true that with the access and ease that the Internet has brought, we have new work habits and transportable offices. As I look ahead 10 years, it is exciting to contemplate what that social studies teacher will be working on at O'Hare, as well as what kind of plane he will be flying in.

Even as these pages are written, our students are growing into adults who will create new solutions to world problems. We owe it to them to join the 21st century and to focus our work. Curriculum mapping not only provides us with a hub for focusing our current efforts, but also provides us with a tool to launch curriculum plans for our students' futures.

Appendixes

Appendix 1	Curriculum Mapping: Mixed-Group and Like-Group Review Protocol

1. In small cross-curricular groups, please complete the items noted on the Curriculum Mapping Response worksheets. This feedback will be used by staff members to develop follow-up sessions so they can work on resolving the gaps, repetitions, and issues that surface during the review process.

2. Divide teachers into cross-curricular groups of five to eight people. Have teachers distribute copies of their maps to others in their small group before the meeting. Teachers in each group are asked to read each other's maps for the following items before they come to the read-through session:

   • "A-ha's"—something they've learned

   • Possible gaps

   • Possible repetitions

   • Questions that are related to items on the curriculum maps and that may need to be addressed

3. Assign each group to a table.

4. Appoint one person to neatly record the information discussed in the group on the Curriculum Mapping Response Sheets.

(continued)

Appendix 1	**Curriculum Mapping: Mixed-Group and Like-Group Review Protocol (*cont.*)**

5. Appoint a facilitator to keep the group on task and to discourage debate. (Keep in mind that the purpose of this process is to identify the questions and the areas that need to be discussed further at a later time.)

6. Appoint a timekeeper to keep the group focused and on task.

7. Using a round-robin format, have the facilitator ask the members of the group to take one minute each and to highlight aspects of their maps.

8. Next, have the facilitator ask the group to focus individually on each person's map and to note feedback about each of the bulleted items in Step 2 above.

9. Ask the recorder to inscribe the responses on large paper. After everyone passes, the facilitator proceeds to the next person's map and repeats the process until everyone's map has been reviewed.

10. After everyone's map has been reviewed, ask the group to discuss the items recorded and to put an asterisk beside the priority areas.

11. Compile the sheets from all groups and give them to the staff to review individually.

12. Have the department- or grade-level groups complete this same process.

13. Make sure that priority areas that have surfaced in the group review process are resolved in the school first, if possible, and then at the district level, if necessary.

Appendix 2	Math District Map/Curriculum Framework

2nd Grade

- Number Concepts
    - ❖ Place Value
        - √√ Identifies the place value to the 100s place
            - √ Compares numbers to 1,000 by counting, reading, writing, and modeling
            - √ Determines ordinals
            - √ Orders through oral or written communication numbers to 100
    - ❖ Rounding
        - √ Rounds to nearest 10

- Computation
    - ❖ Addition
        - √√ Demonstrates automaticity with addition facts to 12
        - √√ Adds two-digit numbers with regrouping
            - √ Computes facts to 18 without manipulatives
            - √ Computes facts to 18 with manipulatives
            - √ Demonstrates fact families through written communication
            - √ Adds multiple addends
    - ❖ Subtraction
        - √√ Demonstrates automaticity with subtraction facts to 12
        - √√ Subtracts two-digit numbers with regrouping
            - √ Computes facts to 18 without manipulatives
            - √ Computes facts to 18 with manipulatives

- Problem Solving
    - √√ Uses appropriate operation from key information
    - √ Computes accurately in problem solving
    - √ Applies strategies such as these:
        - •• draws a picture
        - •• makes a table or graph
        - •• creates a model
        - •• writes a number sentence
        - •• uses manipulatives
    - √ Estimates answers

(continued)

Appendix 2	Math District Map/Curriculum Framework (*cont.*)

- Time
  - ❖ Clock
    - √√ Tells time to five minutes
    - √ Tells time to hour
    - √ Tells time to half hour
  - ❖ Calendar
    - √ Identifies dates, days, and months of events using a calendar

- Money
  - √√ Identifies value of penny, nickel, dime, quarter, half-dollar, and dollar
  - √√ Counts coin combinations to $1.00
  - √ Chooses different coin combinations to show same value
  - √ Determines fewest coins to make an amount

- Measurement
  - √√ Identifies starting point on a ruler
  - √√ Identifies ending point on a ruler
  - √ Uses a ruler to measure inches

- Graphing
  - √ Collects data for chart or graph
  - √ Records data on chart or graph
  - √ Gains information from chart or graph

- Geometry
  - √ Identifies through oral or written communication differences between plane and solid figures

Key:

- •   Core Curriculum
- ❖   Category
- ••   Subcategory
- √√   Benchmark
- √   Critical Skill

Appendix 3	Social Studies District Map/Curriculum Framework

8th Grade

- Economic Production, Distribution, and Consumption
    - ❖ Economic Theories and Practical Economics
        - •• Comparison of the Varying Economic Systems
            - √ Compares and contrasts state-controlled and traditional capitalism (reading skill)
            - √ Synthesizes and evaluates text for main ideas and supporting details (reading skill)
            - √ Compares and contrasts the three basic economic systems
        - •• The Law of Supply and Demand
            - √√ Graphs the Law of Supply and Demand and data pertaining to it
            - √√ Explains how supply and demand affect our economy
            - √ Explains elasticity
            - √ Manipulates and analyzes visual aids with multiple sets of data (reading skill)
            - √ Specifies how supply and demand affect our personal consumption and production
    - ❖ Microeconomics
        - •• Competition and Monopolies
            - √√ Compares and contrasts different business organization types
            - √ Compares and contrasts types of monopolies
            - √ Explains the difference between a monopoly and oligopoly
            - √ Analyzes economic cartoons
            - √ Applies government policies to business
        - •• Advertising and Marketing
            - √√ Designs and develops an ad campaign for a product or service
            - √ Explains marketing and distribution
        - •• American Labor Force
            - √ Demonstrates steps to start a small business
            - √ Explains the purpose of unions
    - ❖ Macroeconomics
        - •• Federal Reserve
            - √√ Explains how the Federal Reserve affects the money supply
            - √ Lists functions of the Federal Reserve

(continued)

Appendix 3	Social Studies District Map/Curriculum Framework (*cont.*)

    •• Money and Banking
      √√ Explains the characteristics of money
       √ Summarizes the history of banking and current bank functions

    •• Global Economics
      √ Explains the increasing rule of global economics and its effect
        on the U.S. economy
      √ Draws connections to world issues (reading skill)
      √ Uses media to understand issues relating to global economics

    •• Controlling Employment and Inflation
      √√ Defines employment and inflation
       √ Interprets the consumer price index
       √ Summarizes the government's role in affecting unemployment

• Individual Groups, Communities, and Institutions
    •• Stock Exchange
      √√ Explains the various parts of a stock report
       √ Identifies components of a stock portfolio
       √ Explains how the Stock Exchange operates
       √ Demonstrates the knowledge of purchasing a stock (the process)

    •• Investing
      √√ Explains and demonstrates the process of investing
       √ Translates the rule of 72

    •• Introduction to the American Economic Systems
      √√ Understands and applies the role of the consumer
      √√ Connects the role of a consumer with personal habits

    •• Housing/Transportation
      √√ Creates strategies for personal budget and credit card management
       √ Demonstrates steps used for buying a house or car
       √ Observes buying strategies and relates to personal life
       √ Examines sources of loans and credit

Key:

    •   Core Curriculum
    ❖   Category
    ••   Subcategory
  √√   Benchmark
   √   Critical Skill

Appendix 4 Northwest Professional Development Model, 2003–2004

	August 14 (Goal Setting and Data Analysis)	August 29 (School Goal Setting and School Improvement Plans)	September 24 (School Goal and Curriculum Focus)	October 15 (Workday)
Essential Questions	1. How can processing these data help Northwest identify strengths and areas of growth? 2. How can we use these data to guide instruction? 3. What goals will make a difference in Northwest student achievement?	1. How can Northwest's processing of these data help us identify strengths and areas of growth? 2. How can we use these data to guide instruction? 3. What goals will make a difference in Northwest student achievement? 4. What action steps are needed? 5. What data and artifacts will be used as evidence of success?	1. How can Northwest use the data from 2002–2003 in planning my instruction to increase student achievement? 2. In my classroom, how can I apply educational research to increase student achievement? 3. In my classroom, how can I apply educational research to meet individual student needs?	1. How can I make sharing student progress with parents meaningful?
Content	• Review 2002–2003 data and priorities in math gathered from data-sharing session in May 2003. • Review 2002–2003 data and priorities in reading gathered from data-sharing session in May 2003.	• School improvement goals for 2003–2004 • Professional development model 2002–2003	• Individual classroom data and school goals • Curriculum maps • *Classroom Instruction That Works: Research-Based Strategies for Increasing Student Achievement* (Marzano, Pollock, & Pickering, 2001)	• Report cards • Conferences
Skills	• Present data and priorities. • Process priorities. • Establish goals for 2003–2004.	• Review and revise professional development model using data and priorities.	• Facilitate grade-level discussion of how to use data to guide instruction.	• Convey social, emotional, and academic area of growth and concern to parents using the reading template, the report card, and the teacher, parent, and child conferences.

(continued)

Skills			• Provide a review of Chapters 1–4 studied last year from *Classroom Instruction That Works.* • Presentation and discussion of *Classroom Instruction That Works,* Chapter 5. • Review the study group's action step for *Classroom Instruction That Works.*	
Evidence	• School improvement goals for math and reading for 2003–2004	• Updated professional development model 2003–2004	• Unit or weekly plans • Notes on Chapters 1–4 from *Classroom Instruction That Works.* • Study guide for thoughtful analysis and use of specific strategies from *Classroom Instruction That Works,* Chapter 5 • Study group time line	• Report cards • Reading template • Portfolios • Anecdotal records • Student-led conferences agenda • Teacher, parent, and child conferences
Time Line/ Deadlines	• August 14, 2003	• August 29, 2003	• September 24, 2003	• October 28, 2003, from 4:00 p.m. to 8:00 p.m. • October 31, 2003, from 8:00 a.m. to 3:00 p.m. • November 4, 2003, from 4:00 p.m. to 8:00 p.m.
Materials to Bring	• Data copies for all certified staff members • Goal planning sheet with priorities from May 2003 • Building improvement goals for 2002–2003	• Data from 2002–2003 • Professional improvement model for 2002–2003	• Copies of *Classroom Instruction That Works* • Student artifacts using Chapters 1–5 strategies from *Classroom Instruction That Works* • Curriculum maps	• Report cards • Reading template • Portfolios • Anecdotal records • Student-led conferences • Teacher, parent, and child conferences

(continued)

Appendix 4   Northwest Professional Development Model, 2003–2004 (*cont.*)

	November 26 (K–12 Vertical Teams, District Agenda)	December 19 (School Goal Focus)	January 21 (School Goal and Curriculum Focus)	February 19 (K–12 Vertical Teams, District Agenda)
Essential Questions		1. How can I create a quality map with alignment and integration of specified skills and enter it on Techpath? 2. How can I apply educational research in my classroom to improve student achievement? 3. Using the pretest data from the problem-solving test, how can I help my students grow in problem-solving strategies that are most likely to improve their achievement? 4. Using data from the fall reading assessments and report card reading benchmarks, how can I help my students grow in reading strategies that are most likely to improve their achievement?	1. How can I create a quality map with alignment and integration of specified skills and enter it on Techpath? 2. How can I apply educational research in my classroom to improve student achievement in problem solving and reading?	
Content		• Techpath information on rollover • Map alignment seminar for staff members who are new to the district (open to all staff members who would like to attend)	• Techpaths • Curriculum maps • *Classroom Instruction That Works*, Chapters 8–9	

(continued)

Content	• *Classroom Instruction That Works*, Chapters 6–7 • Review of fall reading assessment and problem-solving data	
Skills	• Provide coaching questions for quality cell. • Provide assistance in creating maps. • Provide training for map rollover into Techpaths. • Present and discuss *Classroom Instruction That Works*, Chapters 6–7. • Provide assistance with data interpretation and achievement and individual class goal setting.	• Continue to facilitate the entering of curriculum maps on Techpaths. • Present and discuss *Classroom Instruction That Works*, Chapters 8–9.
Evidence	• Fall assessment data • Curriculum maps • Coaching handouts • Techpaths program • Study guide for thoughtful analysis and use of specific strategies from *Classroom Instruction That Works*, Chapters 6–7 • Copies of *Classroom Instruction That Works*	• Copies of *Classroom Instruction That Works* • Study guide for thoughtful analysis and use of specific strategies from *Classroom Instruction That Works*, Chapters 8–9 • Curriculum maps • Techpaths program
Time Line/ Deadlines	• Math and social studies maps aligned and integrated in specified areas and on Techpaths by March 29, 2004	• Math and social studies maps aligned and on Techpaths by March 29, 2004

(continued)

Appendix 4   Northwest Professional Development Model, 2003–2004 (*cont.*)

	March 19 (District or School Curriculum Focus)	April 22 (District or School Curriculum Focus)	May 12 (School Goal Focus)	May 26 (School Goal Setting and School Improvement Plans)
Essential Questions	1. How can I create quality maps with alignment and integration of specific skills? 2. How can I apply educational research in my classroom to improve student achievement?	1. How can I apply educational research in my classroom to improve student achievement? 2. If I use data from the winter reading assessments and the report card reading and math benchmarks, how can I help my students grow in reading strategies that are most likely to improve their achievement?	1. How can processing Iowa Test for Basic Skills (ITBS) data in reading comprehension and math help us identify strengths and areas of growth? 2. How can processing the spring problem-solving test and reading assessment data help us identify strengths and areas of growth?	1. How can processing these data help us identify strengths and areas of growth? 2. How can we use these data to guide instruction for 2004–2005?
Materials to Bring		• Individual curriculum maps • Individual classroom goals that speak to achieving Northwest school goals • Student artifacts using Chapters 6–7 strategies from *Classroom Instruction That Works* • List of integrated topics	• Student artifacts using Chapters 8–9 strategies from *Classroom Instruction That Works* • Curriculum maps • List of integrated topics	
Time Line/Deadlines		• Language arts and science on Techpaths by March 29, 2004 • Special area and special education maps on Techpaths per department expectations by March 29, 2004	• Language arts and science on Techpaths by March 29, 2004 • Special area and special education maps on Techpaths per department expectations by March 29, 2004	

(continued)

Essential Questions	Content	Skills	Evidence
3. If I use data from the winter reading assessments and the report card reading benchmarks, how can I help my students grow in reading strategies that are most likely to improve their achievement? 4. How can I help my students grow in problem-solving strategies that are most likely to improve their achievement?	• *Classroom Instruction That Works*, Chapters 10–11 • Curriculum maps • Techpaths • Review of winter reading assessment data	• Continue to facilitate the entering of curriculum maps on Techpaths. • Present and discuss *Classroom Instruction That Works*, Chapters 10–11. • Provide assistance with data interpretation and individual class goal setting.	• Winter reading assessment data and report card benchmark data
3. How can I help my students grow in problem-solving strategies that are most likely to improve their achievement?	• *Classroom Instruction That Works*, Chapters 12–13 • Problem-solving strategy bank	• Present and discuss *Classroom Instruction That Works*, Chapters 12–13. • Present problem-solving strategy bank.	• Study guide for thoughtful analysis and use of specific strategies of *Classroom Instruction That Works*, Chapter 12–13
	• Data-sharing of ITBS reading comprehension and math • Data-sharing of problem-solving test and reading assessment	• Present data. • Process data. • Record feedback.	• Feedback sheets
3. How can we use these data to write a relevant professional development model for 2004–2005?	• Data • Professional development model revision	• Process feedback for common threads. • Review and revise professional development model for 2004–2005 using data and feedback.	• Updated professional model

(continued)

Appendix 4 Northwest Professional Development Model, 2003–2004 (cont.)

Evidence	• Copies of *Classroom Instruction That Works* • Techpaths • Curriculum maps • Study guide for thoughtful analysis and use of specific strategies from *Classroom Instruction That Works*, Chapters 10–11	• Copies of problem-solving strategy bank for all certified staff members		
Time Line/Deadlines	• Math and social studies themes maps aligned and integrated in specified areas and on Techpaths by March 29, 2004 • Language arts and science on Techpaths by March 29, 2004 • Special area and special education maps on Techpaths per department expectations by March 29, 2004	• April 22, 2004	• May 12, 2004	• May 26, 2004
Materials to Bring	• Copies of *Classroom Instruction That Works* • Student artifacts using strategies from Chapters 10–11 in *Classroom Instruction That Works* • Techpaths • Curriculum maps	• Student artifacts using strategies from Chapter 12 in *Classroom Instruction That Works* • Copies of *Classroom Instruction That Works* • Copies of problem-solving strategy bank for all certified staff members	• Data copies for all certified staff members • Feedback sheet for strengths and areas of growth	• Feedback sheets for all certified staff members • School improvement plan • Data • Highlighters

Appendix 5	Frequently Asked Questions and Answers

As Minnehaha Academy in Minneapolis, Minnesota, implemented mapping, the academy's administrators and teachers had questions and concerns. The following questions and the answers provided by Stephen O'Neil may be helpful as you implement curriculum mapping.

Administrative Questions

Q. *Is technology necessary to successfully implement curriculum mapping? If so, what types of technology best support curriculum mapping?*

A. A school can implement curriculum mapping without technology, even using the paper-and-pencil approach. Curriculum mapping without a computer would still be beneficial. Technology, however, provides important features, such as accessibility, ability to easily edit, and an opportunity to view other teachers' curriculum quickly. The technology can be created in-house using a variety of software applications, including *FileMaker® Pro* and *Microsoft® Access*. If we choose to create our own software, we should follow the KISS principle ("Keep It Simple, Stupid") and should make it user friendly. There are also several curriculum mapping software databases that can be purchased or subscribed to for an annual fee.

Q. *How do you suggest sustaining the momentum of curriculum mapping when new faculty members are hired each school year?*

A. New faculty is one of the greatest challenges facing those responsible for the curriculum mapping initiative. It is vital to provide training to new teachers during their orientation and throughout their first school year as part of an induction program. They need not only the training in the "why" and "how" of curriculum mapping, but also the technology training. I have found it helpful to talk about our curriculum mapping work during interviews.

Q. *How do you create a time line for the curriculum mapping initiative?*

A. Every school needs to create a time line that works best for it. No one formula best suits all schools. We chose to use a three-year curriculum mapping cycle. I sometimes wonder if we attempted too much during the first year while mapping the entire curriculum, but there were substantial benefits. When you take on one or two subjects at a time, you do not have the same opportunity to find interdisciplinary connecting points across disciplines, and there is a potential to lose momentum for the entire initiative. The key was providing the time for our faculty members to map their curriculum.

(continued)

Appendix 5	**Frequently Asked Questions and Answers (*cont.*)**

Q. *What constitutes "critical mass" in terms of support needed for curriculum mapping?*

A. A school's administration must throw its full weight behind a curriculum mapping project. Administrators need to model genuine enthusiasm for the initiative. More important, they must make it a high priority to provide time for faculty members to work on curriculum mapping and to make it a focal point for the school. Mapping cannot become just another add-on. In regards to faculty support of the initiative, I generally follow the 60/30/10 principle: If 60 percent of the faculty supports it, 30 percent will mildly support it but professionally get on board, and 10 percent will go kicking and screaming; then a school is on target to move forward.

Q. *How can curriculum mapping connect with other comprehensive school initiatives and create greater efficiency?*

A. During the past several years at Minnehaha Academy, we have focused on areas including writing types across character education, curriculum, diversity, faith and learning, and technology and curriculum. Oftentimes, the task forces or committees working on those types of initiatives will unintentionally disconnect curriculum from their work or will discuss it outside using a review model. Curriculum mapping provides an avenue where teachers can streamline these important initiatives through the curriculum rather than working the initiatives in parallel with the curriculum. We are able to comprehensively examine the preschool through grade 12 experience; to examine the grade-level experience with each initiative; and to inspect the scaffolding of content, skills, and assessments. With curriculum mapping, we have the opportunity to assess and make changes to our curriculum in all of our initiative areas.

Q. *Does curriculum mapping take the place of the curriculum review cycle?*

A. Curriculum mapping *becomes* the review cycle. There is no longer a need to conduct a review separate from curriculum mapping. The review phases provide a natural opportunity to examine and edit the school's curriculum.

Faculty Questions

Q. *How much information should I include on my curriculum map? Where should my map fall on the spectrum of most broad to most detailed?*

A. On the one hand, a faculty member should not include so little that a reader of the map is unable to understand the content, skills, and assessments of a subject. Enough information should be provided to be helpful to all readers. On the other hand, too

(continued)

Appendix 5	**Frequently Asked Questions and Answers (*cont.*).**

much information can be burdensome to the writer and reader. For example, providing every vocabulary word for a language arts class might err on the side of providing too much detail. The rule of thumb I use with faculty members on their first draft is they should develop the map while keeping in mind the needs of the faculty reader or the type of search a faculty member would conduct while using the database.

Q. *What does the term "rough draft" mean as it relates to the first edition of my curriculum map?*

A. Some teachers feel general anxiety about writing a rough draft. They want their first draft to be a final product. Each person needs to recognize that future drafts will occur, especially during the review process. There is no need to belabor a first draft when subsequent drafts will be required. I also encourage faculty members to map what they really do in the classroom, not what they wish they did. If they try to edit as they write, the mapping assignment becomes more challenging than it needs to be, and it may not represent reality.

Q. *Who is the audience that will read my curriculum map?*

A. Each school needs to decide. It seems, at a minimum, that the entire faculty should have the ability to view each teacher's curriculum. It also seems natural to allow students to view the curriculum maps; however, it should be noted whether students are viewing a draft version or a final version. Finally, a school should decide whether its parent community should have access to all the curriculum maps or to only the curriculum maps of their students' teachers. In this instance, parents should view only final versions. Showing parents curriculum maps allows parents to partner with faculty members to best serve the students.

Q. *When more than one faculty member teaches the same course or class, how should each faculty member map the curriculum?*

A. I strongly suggest that each faculty member map independently unless faculty members have historically worked together to develop and implement curriculum. In that case, I would allow the handful of faculty members to map their shared curriculum together. It is important to remember that curriculum mapping is a tool to show the curriculum reality in the classroom, not to develop a new curriculum and then map it.

Q. *How often can a curriculum map be edited during the review process?*

A. We agreed to use the curriculum maps that existed at the beginning of each school year. The maps used during the review process came from that preestablished time.

(continued)

Appendix 5	**Frequently Asked Questions and Answers (*cont.*)**

Individual maps can be edited during the review process, especially as teachers notice natural changes that should occur. At Minnehaha Academy, I have considered archiving the curriculum maps for each school year so I can show progress and can note changes over time.

Q. *Because curriculum mapping is a substantial initiative, how will we find the time to do this well?*

A. It is imperative that administrators find time for their faculty members. Otherwise, faculty members will see curriculum mapping as just one more "thing on my plate." Using the faculty and department meeting time and the professional development days will be great ways to provide time. Providing substitutes, release time, or summer curriculum development compensation can be other excellent ways to show that curriculum mapping is important and a priority for your school.

Q. *Are essential questions a necessary part of curriculum mapping?*

A. No. Curriculum mapping can be successfully accomplished without using essential questions, but their absence may inhibit complete curriculum renewal, particularly with an individual teacher's curriculum. However, many faculty members find such questions quite helpful in their mapping efforts as they align those essential questions with their curriculum's content, skills, and assessments. Several faculty members at Minnehaha Academy felt that without essential questions they would not have been enthusiastic about moving forward with curriculum mapping. I do not believe essential questions should be a requirement for curriculum mapping but rather should be strongly encouraged.

Q. *Why are we doing curriculum mapping? Will it really serve a purpose?*

A. Improved curricular communication is the primary reason to use curriculum mapping. It provides an opportunity to view all teachers' curricula. With curriculum mapping, a school doesn't begin with the end in mind and then make changes to bring about that end. It begins with the current reality and builds toward the vision. In this way, there is greater ownership in this grassroots movement. It is a more natural process. If all curriculum decisions are made with the best interests of the students in mind, a school must begin with an examination of the real curriculum. Only then can the curriculum best be renewed.

Appendix 6	Checklist for Curriculum Mapping

I. Gain information.
____ Select a format for gathering information and a plan for training.
____ Record data on maps. Use plan books or other forms of data, not page numbers. Use verbs to denote skills and nouns to show assessments.
____ Use the school calendar year to record data, such as August–June.
____ Individual teachers should place their content, skills, and assessment information on a map.

II. After data are recorded on the teacher maps, connect all maps or review maps on the computer.
____ From all grade levels in your school, design a way for all teachers to review the maps for processing.

III. Read the first drafts.
The first read-through is with the teacher as editor. This step is done alone!
____ Have each teacher read all the maps and act as an editor.
____ Edit for repetitions. Recognize the difference between repetition and redundancy. Spiraling is the goal. (For example, repeated family trees need to go.)
____ Edit for gaps in content, thinking processes, skills, and assessments. For example, in the measurement strand, what is being taught and what is missing? Where in the map do you find measuring to 1/16 of an inch?
____ Make a note of new findings (that is, what your colleagues are teaching, and so on). Where do you see possibilities for integrating the curriculum?
____ As you look at the big picture, look for long-term revisions (that is, areas that will affect other grade levels or schools).

IV. Start reviewing the mixed small group.
All grade levels are represented. Teachers should not work with their regular instructional team. Share individual findings. (No more than six to eight teachers should be in this group.)
____ Have someone record the findings for use at next step.
____ No revisions are suggested.

V. Determine areas for immediate revision.
This step involves large groups or job-alike groups.
____ Use information from the review by the mixed small group. Identify areas that can be handled with relative ease. Make needed changes. Delete repetitions and fill gaps where possible.

(continued)

Appendix 6	Checklist for Curriculum Mapping (*cont.*)

___ Determine a timetable for action.

___ Determine if research is needed in an area.

___ Create a consensus map for the course of study.

VI. Make sure local and state standards or objectives are included!

___ Determine where you are requiring mastery of concepts or skills.

___ Look to see that each grade level contributes to mastery (that is, if 4th grade shows a benchmark in the mastery of multiplication, grades 3 and below need to show work in that area on their maps).

___ Hint: Look at your state test to determine what skills need to be taught. These skills must be taught at least two months before testing. If testing is done in April, you agree that all new skills will be introduced by the end of February, which gives time for practice. This schedule does not mean that new skills won't be taught after February. Remember, this is a spiraling curriculum.

PLEASE NOTE: All maps need to be reviewed periodically. Now is a good time to establish curriculum review committees or cabinets at the site and district.

Next, move on to continued planning and renewal. Use technology to record and collect data. Technology can make the revision process move smoothly and quickly.

NOTE: You are not through mapping—the cycle continues!

Source: Based on work by Heidi Hayes Jacobs; prepared by Mary Ann Holt.

| **Appendix 7** | **Curriculum Map Information Sheet for the First Read-Through** |

Part 1

Please complete a review form for EACH map in your packet.

Department: _____   Date: _____

Course: _____   Reader: _____

Procedure for Each Subject Map

First Look: You are reading for information to see the big picture of what is taught in our curriculum. Please record anything that surprises you—the Wows!!—things you didn't know were happening in the Maryville High School curriculum.

Analysis: In this reading, you will be looking for learning connections from content to skills to assessment. Is it clear to you what students should know and be able to do and how they demonstrate their learning? Can you see student progress from fundamental knowledge and skills to more sophisticated levels? Please record any comments or questions.

(continued)

Appendix 7	**Curriculum Map Information Sheet for the First Read-Through (*cont.*)**

Integration: On the map itself, underline or circle in colored pencil or pen places that you think are areas for integration with other courses or departments and **indicate the connection**.

Assessment: Read the assessment section of the map, and check off the types of formal assessment listed:

- Objective quizzes/tests (short answer/commercial/ teacher-made, and so on.) _____

- Oral (debate, speech, group discussions, reading aloud, and so on) _____

- Projects _____

- Problem-based (complex question/task/issue to be resolved through inquiry) _____

- Performance (skit, presentation, musical piece, and so on) _____

- Portfolios _____

- Exhibitions _____

- Learning logs or journals _____

- Written assessments (these, essay, report, and so on) _____

- Research paper _____

- Other (please list type of assessment) _____

(continued)

Appendix 7	**Curriculum Map Information Sheet for the First Read-Through (*cont.*)**

Technology: Please record how technology is used in this course.

_____

_____

_____

_____

_____

Summary: Please record any general comments, questions, or recommendations you have which relate to information contained in this map.

Reader Comments/Questions/Recommendations

(continued)

| Appendix 7 | **Curriculum Map Information Sheet for the First Read-Through (*cont.*)** |

Part 2

Please complete a review form for EACH map in your packet.

Department: _____   Reader: _____

As the reader or reviewer, you are now looking for possible learning gaps or redundancies in content or skills. Redundancy is repetition of the same thing in the same way. Students need repeated practice, but the manner in which they practice should differ in form and should be designed to move the student toward deeper levels of understanding.

It may be helpful, where applicable, to first read course-alike maps (all Spanish 1, for example) and then to read maps in sequence (Spanish 1, 2, 3, 4, for example). Please record your observations in the space provided.

Reviewer Comments/Questions/Recommendations

Course(s)	Possible Gaps Noted	Possible Repetitions/ Redundancies

Note: Include this form in your map packet.

Appendix 8 · Elementary Principals' Reading Professional Development

	September 20	November 8	January 17	March 14	May 9
Essential Questions	• What makes a quality-guided reading lesson? • How do I provide appropriate feedback after an observation?	• What is balanced literacy? Is it different at different grades? • How does guided reading fit into balanced literacy?	• What is comprehension? • How does retelling hook to comprehension? • What do each of the benchmark assessments tell us?	• How do you teach writing? • What are the components of an effective writing program?	• How do we best serve the less-proficient readers in our district?
Content	• Guided Reading – definition – quality lesson – coaching questions	• Balanced Literacy – definition or components – application – coaching questions – guided reading's role	• Comprehension – definition – retelling • Benchmark Assessments – understanding assessments	• Writing Process – definition – components – application – coaching questions	• Title I/ Supplemental Reading – purpose – program – criteria to qualify
Skills	• Define guided reading. • Identify components of a quality-guided reading lesson. • Create a checklist for guided reading observation. • Create coaching questions after observing a guided reading lesson.	• Define balanced literacy. • Identify components of balanced literacy. • Connect application of balanced literacy to various grade levels. • Define the role of guided reading in balanced literacy.	• Define comprehension. • Define retelling. • Describe benchmark assessment components.	• Define the writing process. • Identify components of the writing process. • Connect reading and writing. • Define the role of writing in balanced literacy. • Create coaching questions for teachers about the writing process.	• Define Title I/ Supplemental Reading. • Demonstrate an understanding of the criteria for qualifying for the program. • Identify ways to support associates.

(continued)

Appendix 8   Elementary Principals' Reading Professional Development (*cont.*)

Skills	• Identify when to move children to a new guided reading level.	• Create coaching question for teachers about balanced literacy.			
Follow-up	• Two teacher observations and copy of feedback conference as it relates to guided reading	• Two teacher observations and copy of feedback conference as it relates to balanced literacy	• Three student assessments for January benchmark with grade level that each is assigned to (classroom teacher supervision?)	• Use small group discussion, maybe one per grade level, around the writing process, implementation in the school, questions, suggestions, and so on. • Provide feedback to Jan and Jennie (writing committee).	• Follow up with all kindergarten, and grades 1, 2, and 3 teachers so telephone calls to parents for qualifying students are made before school is out.
Notes	• Model lesson for principals	• Review guided reading assignment. • Model coaching a teacher about balanced literacy.	• Penny activity • Assessment protocols	• Show examples of study work.	• Log for teachers to use to verify phone calls

Appendix 9 · A High School Staff Development Plan, 2001–2002

	September 19 (District Focus)	September 26 (Study Groups)	October 17 (School Focus)	October 24 (Study Groups Voluntary)	November 2 (School Focus)
Essential Questions	• How can curriculum mapping be used as a tool to integrate the various initiatives being worked on by the district?	• What are the functions of the Any High School (AHS) immediate student action (ISA) program?	• How do the results of the math and reading assessments from the spring of 2001 affect Any High School curriculum? • What graduation requirements should be in place for an Any High School student?		• What graduation requirements should be in place for an Any High School student? • How can faculty and staff become more sensitive in dealing with the diverse needs of our students?
Content	• Connections activity • District goals • School goals • Secondary curriculum goals • Curriculum map cell (quality)	• Purpose of the ISA program • Description of the ISA program • Data from reading assessment • Classroom teacher's role in the ISA program	• Strands, benchmarks, and skills • Integration of reading, research, and technology • Common assessments • Alignment of assessments with benchmarks • Data from math and reading assessments • Any High School graduation requirements	• CPR training	• Any High School graduation requirements • Student gender preferences

(continued)

Appendix 9   A High School Staff Development Plan, 2001–2002 (*cont.*)

Skills	• Explain and relate connections to "big picture" and the mapping process. • Consider how mapping is a communication tool and systems process. • Review building and district goals. • Review curriculum goals, and identify what they specifically mean for AHS. • Share staff development plan for understanding of time line. • Model the curriculum map cell to improve quality of maps. • Apply quality cell strategy, and work on maps.	• To understand the purpose of the ISA program at AHS • To use strategies suggested by ISA team to meet student needs	• Examine and refine strands and skills to ensure they are increasing in difficulty. • Revise frameworks to reflect changes. • Align terminology in skills for consistency. • Integrate reading and problem-solving skills and strategies into the frameworks. • Align benchmarks with specific assessments. • Examine graduation requirements that are in place for AHS students. • Revise AHS graduation requirements.	• Examine graduation requirements that are in place for AHS students. • Revise AHS graduation requirements. • Consider how a student struggling with gender preference might experience daily life at AHS.
Evidence	• Captured information from activity • One to two cells completed and submitted to school's curriculum facilitators	• Teachers using strategies with students in ISA program	• Strands updated to reflect scaffolded skills • Framework updated • Integration of reading and problem-solving reflected in frameworks • Alignment matrixes completed • Graduation requirements to be refined and revised	• Graduation requirements will be refined and revised.

(continued)

	November 14 (Building Focus)	November 28 (Building Focus)	December 21 (Teacher Work Day)	January 14 (Study Groups)	January 16 (District Focus)	February 20 (District Focus)
Time Line/Deadlines	1:05 p.m.–2:05 p.m. Jennie Johnson 2:05 p.m.–2:35 p.m. Gary Ratigan 2:35 p.m.–3:20 p.m. Work in rooms	• Early bird through fifth hour as assigned	TBD		• Early bird through fifth hour as assigned	1:05 p.m.–2:05 p.m. Gary Ratigan/John Schumacher 2:05 p.m.–2:15 p.m. Pop Break 2:15 p.m.–3:15 p.m. Gary Ratigan/John Schumacher
Materials to Bring	• Resource notebooks • Frameworks from Web • Maps	• No materials necessary	• Resource notebooks • Frameworks from Web • Maps • Curriculum guides			• Curriculum guides
Essential Questions		• How can reading strategies be integrated into the curriculum map?		• What do teachers need to do in preparation for the student, parent, and advisor (SPA) conference?		
Content	• Curriculum map cell (integration of vocabulary, inferential skills, problem-solving skills) • Quality coaching checklist or rubric	• Reading strategies • Curriculum map cells		• Components of SPA conference • SPA materials	• Read-through using questions that connect to the goals (see read-through process)	• Strands, benchmarks, and skills • Integration of reading, research, and technology • Common assessments • Alignment of assessments with benchmarks

(continued)

Appendix 9	A High School Staff Development Plan, 2001–2002 (cont.)				
Skills	• Model the integration strategy for reading and problem-solving skills. • Use a peer coach for quality-coaching checklist or rubric. • Integrate reading and problem-solving strategies or skills on curriculum map(s).	• Integrate reading strategies or skills on curriculum map(s).	• Prepare for SPA conference. • Confirm SPA conference schedule.	• Divide into mixed teams of 6–8 teachers from different levels and subjects. • Read through maps using protocol for school's goals. • Conduct read-throughs. • Set priorities for feedback: check individual, check team, check school. • Identify areas of focus. • Disseminate data to staff.	• Examine and refine strands and skills to ensure they are increasing in difficulty. • Revise frameworks to reflect changes. • Align terminology in skills for consistency. • Integrate reading and problem-solving skills and strategies into the frameworks. • Align benchmarks with specific assessments.
Evidence	• Map(s) that reflect integration strategies/skills completed and submitted to school's curriculum facilitators	• Curriculum maps will be integrated with reading strategies.	• Faculty members will conduct successful SPA conferences with each student whom they advise.	• Data with priority areas marked and turned in to Gary Ratigan. • Compiled data shared with staff members	• Strands updated and reflect scaffolded skills • Framework updated • Integrations of reading and problem solving reflected in frameworks • Alignment matrixes completed

(continued)

Timeline/Deadlines	TBD	• Early bird through fifth hour as assigned	TBD	• Early bird through fifth hour as assigned	TBD
Materials to Bring	• Curriculum map cells • Resource notebooks • Frameworks from Web • Maps • Curriculum guides	• Curriculum maps • Reading strategies		• Resource notebooks • Frameworks from Web • Maps • Maps from your mixed group	• Resource notebooks • Frameworks from Web • Maps

	February 27 (School Focus)	March 13 (School Focus)	March 27 (Study Groups)	April 17 (District Focus)	April 24 (District Focus)	May 15 (School Focus)
Essential Questions	• How should the data from the Iowa Test of Educational Development (ITED) be used to improve student achievement? • What does the data from the ITED tell us?	• What are the goals of the district reading, writing, and problem-solving committees as they pertain to AHS?	• What are the graduation requirement recommendations that should be presented to the school board? • What modifications need to be made to our school's improvement plan?		• What reading strategies have been used in AHS this year, and how have they helped improve student performance?	

(continued)

Appendix 9　A High School Staff Development Plan, 2001–2002 (cont.)

Content		• Reading committee report • Writing committee report • Problem-solving committee report	• AHS revised graduation requirements • School improvement plan	• District data analysis: ITED data, reading assessment, problem-solving assessment, and science assessment • Goal development • Topics for June workshop	• Content-specific reading strategies	• 2002–2003 advisement curriculum • 2002–2003 scheduling concerns
Skills	• Examine and analyze the 2001 ITED test results. • Determine next steps on the basis of the data.	• Review the purposes of the three district committees. • Discuss the effect the committee recommendations will have on AHS.	• Review the revised graduation requirements. • Review the revised school improvement plan as it relates to the comprehensive school improvement plan.	• Review data to determine areas that need to be addressed. • Identify priority areas and set goals. • Identify staff development needs.	• Review reading strategies used by AHS staff members in their specific disciplines. • Share strategies that may be useful to other staff members.	• Plan and prepare for 2002–2003 advisement. • Discuss any concerns or issues regarding the scheduling process for 2002–2003.
Evidence	• Building goals and action plans for 2002–2003 will reflect needs identified in the data.	• Recommendations of the three district committees will be integrated into the building plan.	• Graduation requirements will reflect suggested changes. • 2002–2003 school improvement plan will reflect the suggested revisions.	• Priority areas list • Draft list of goals • Draft list of staff development needs	• Individual curriculum maps will reflect effective reading strategies.	• The 2002–2003 advisement curriculum will reflect suggested changes. • Scheduling for 2002–2003 will reflect any suggested revisions.

(continued)

Time Line/ Deadlines	• Early bird through fifth hour as assigned	TBD		TBD	• Early bird through fifth hour as assigned
Materials to Bring			• School's improvement plan • Graduation requirements	• Resource notebooks • Frameworks from Web • Maps	• Reading strategies • Curriculum maps

Time Line/ Deadlines	TBD
Materials to Bring	• 2002–2003 scheduling time line • 2002–2003 advisement calendar

Curriculum Mapping Resources

Online

Center for Curriculum Mapping. Retrieved December 11, 2003, from http://www.curriculumdesigners.com.

Jacobs, H. H. (2004). Curriculum Designers, Inc. Available at http://www.curriculumdesigners.com.

New York Academy of Sciences: Science Research Program. (2003). Retrieved September 10, 2003, from http://www.nyas.org/education/asr.cfm.

PBS TeacherLine: Course on curriculum mapping. Retrieved September 10, 2003, from http://teacherline.pbs.org/teacherline/.

Verbs and Products for Independent Study (based on Bloom's taxonomy). Engine-Uity, Ltd. Retrieved September 12, 2003, from http://www.engine-uity.com/.

Videotape

Association for Supervision and Curriculum Development (Producer). (1999). *Curriculum mapping: Charting the course for curriculum content.* [Videotape] (Available from the Association for Supervision and Curriculum Development, 1703 North Beauregard Street, Alexandria, VA 22311.)

Mapping Software

The Curriculum Mapper. Westjam Enterprises: Westmont, IL. Retrieved June 22, 2004, from http://www .curriculum mapper.com.

Rubicon Atlas. Atlas Management: Portland, OR. Retrieved June 22, 2004, from http://www.rubiconatlas.com.

TechPaths. TechPaths: Guilford, CT. Retrieved June 22, 2004, from http://www.techpaths.com.

Bibliography

Bloom, B., Enhgelhart, M., Furst, E., Hill, W., & Krathwohl, D. (1956). *The taxonomy of educational objectives. Handbook 1: Cognitive domain*. New York: David McKay.

Boisot, Max. (1998). *Knowledge assets: Securing competitive advantage in the information economy*. New York: Oxford University Press.

Burns, R. C. (2002). Interdisciplinary teamed instruction. In Julie Klein (Ed.), *Interdisciplinary education in K–12 and college*. New York: The College Board.

Costa, A. L., & Garmston, R. J. (1994). *Cognitive coaching: A foundation for renaissance schools*. Norwood, MA: Christopher-Gordon Publishers, Inc.

Costa, A. L., & Kallick, B. (2000). *Habits of mind: A developmental series*. Alexandria, VA: Association for Supervision and Curriculum Development.

English, F. W., & Steffy, B. E. (2001). *Deep curriculum alignment*. Lanham, MD: Scarecrow Press.

Erickson, H. L. (1998). *Concept-based curriculum and instruction*. Alexandria, VA: Association for Supervision and Curriculum Development.

Friedberg, J., & Fedolfi, C. (2001). *Curriculum mapping action priority*. Cambridge, MA: Co-Nect Courier Companies, Inc.

Glickman, C. (2003a). *Democracy and American schools*. Alexandria, VA: Association for Supervision and Curriculum Development.

Glickman, C. (2003b). *Holding sacred ground: Essays on leadership, courage, and endurance in our schools*. New York: Jossey-Bass.

Hamel, G., & Prahalad, C. K. (1994). *Competing for the future*. Cambridge, MA: Harvard Business School Press.

Jacobs, H. H. (1989). *Interdisciplinary curriculum: Design and implementation*. Alexandria, VA: Association for Supervision and Curriculum Development.

Jacobs, H. H. (1997a). *Mapping the big picture: Integrating curriculum and assessment K–12.* Alexandria, VA: Association for Supervision and Curriculum Development.

Jacobs, H. H. (1997b). Redefining assessment. *Social Studies Handbook on Alternative Assessment.* Boston, MA: Prentice Hall.

Jacobs, H. H. (1998, Spring). Connections, mapping, and structures for learning. *NAIS Independent School Magazine.*

Jacobs, H. H. (2000a, Summer). Focus on curriculum mapping. ASCD *Curriculum Handbook*, pp. a–d.

Jacobs, H. H. (2000b). Upgrading the K-12 journey through curriculum mapping. *Knowledge Quest, 29*(2), 25–29.

Jacobs, H. H. (2001). New trends in curriculum: An interview with Heidi Hayes Jacobs. *NAIS Independent School Magazine: Curriculum Conundrum*, 18–22.

Jacobs, H. H. (2003). Connecting curriculum mapping and technology: Digital forms aid data analysis and decision making. *ASCD Curriculum Technology Quarterly, 12*(3), 1–3.

Kercheval, A., & Newbill, S. L. (2001). *A case study of key effective practices in Ohio's improved school districts.* Bloomington, IN: Indiana Center for Evaluation, Smith Research.

Klein, J. T. (1996). *Crossing boundaries: Knowledge, disciplinarities, and interdisciplinarities.* Charlottesville, VA: University of Virginia Press.

Langer, G. A., Colton, A. B., & Goff, L. S. (2003). *Collaborative analysis of student work: Improving teaching and learning.* Alexandria, VA: Association for Supervision and Curriculum Development.

Marzano, R. J. (1992). *A different kind of classroom: Teaching with dimensions of learning.* Alexandria, VA: Association for Supervision and Curriculum Development.

Marzano, R. J. (2000). *Transforming classroom grading.* Alexandria, VA: Association for Supervision and Curriculum Development.

Marzano, R. J., Pollock, J. E., & Pickering, D. J. (2001). *Classroom instruction that works: Research-based strategies for increasing student achievement.*

Alexandria, VA: Association for Supervision and Curriculum Development.

National Association of Independent Schools. (2001, Fall). New trends in curriculum: An interview with Heidi Hayes Jacobs. *Independent School Magazine: Curriculum Conundrum, 61*(1), 18–22.

Nonaka, I., & Takeuchi, H. (1995). *Knowledge creation.* New York: Oxford University Press.

Ohio State Department of Education. (2001). *Office of regional school improvement services: A case study of key effective practices in Ohio's improved school districts.* Bloomington, IN: Indiana Center for Evaluation, Smith Research.

Ohio Statewide Administrators Conference. (2001). *Strategies used by Ohio schools to increase achievement: Highlights from a case study of key effective practices in school districts.* Bloomington, IN: Indiana Center for Evaluation, Smith Research.

Ouchi, W. G. (2003). *Making schools work: A revolutionary plan to get your children the education they need.* New York: Simon and Schuster.

Probasco-Sowers, J. (2001, October 17). Mapping assists teachers. *Des Moines Register*, pp. 1, 6.

Schlecty, P. (1993, Fall). On the frontier of school reform with trailblazers, pioneers, and settlers. *Journal of Staff Development, 14*(4).

Tomlinson, C. (1999). *The differentiated classroom: Responding to the needs of all learners.* Alexandria, VA: Association for Supervision and Curriculum Development.

Udelhofen, S., & Larson, K. (2002). *The mentoring year: A step-by-step guide to professional development.* Phoenix, AZ: All Star Publishing.

Wiggins, G., & McTighe, J. (1998). *Understanding by design.* Alexandria, VA: Association for Supervision and Curriculum Development.

Zmuda, A., Kuklis, R., & Kline, E. (2004). *Transforming schools: creating a culture of continuous improvement.*

Index

Page numbers followed by an *f* indicate a reference to a figure.

About the Authors

H. Lynn Erickson is a private consultant who assists schools and districts around the country with curriculum design and instruction. During the past eight years, she has worked extensively with K–12 teachers and administrators across the country on the design of classroom- and district-level curricula that are aligned to academic standards. She is the author of two bestselling books: *Stirring the Head, Heart, and Soul: Redefining Curriculum and Instruction, 2nd ed.* (2001), and *Concept-Based Curriculum and Instruction: Teaching Beyond the Facts* (2002) by Corwin Press Publishers.

Mary Ann Holt is an independent curriculum consultant who is involved with Dr. Heidi Hayes Jacobs in curriculum mapping and in developing integrated curriculum design. She has worked with hundreds of schools and districts throughout the United States as they focus on issues and practices related to mapping, curriculum integration, and standards. She also served as a principal, classroom teacher, and director of curriculum and instruction, and as a consultant on basic skills for the Tennessee Department of Education. The Chattanooga School for the Liberal Arts, where she last served as principal, is featured on the ASCD tape set, "Curriculum Mapping: Charting the Course for Content." She can be contacted at holt.am@mindspring.com.

Heidi Hayes Jacobs is president of Curriculum Designers, Inc., and director of the Center for Curriculum Mapping. She consults extensively to schools, national and international organizations, media companies, businesses, and nonprofit groups. She has served as an adjunct associate professor at Columbia University's Teachers College in New York City since 1981. ASCD has published her two previous books, *Interdisciplinary Curriculum: Design and Implementation* (1989) and *Mapping the Big Picture: Integrating Curriculum and Assessment K–12* (1997). She is based in Rye, New York, and can be contacted at her Web site, http://www .curriculumdesigners.com, or by e-mail at curricDES@aol.com.

Ann Johnson is the associate superintendent of instruction at Ankeny Community School District in Ankeny, Iowa. Dr. Johnson was previously a consultant in curriculum, assessment, and instruction at an educational intermediate agency in North Central Iowa. Before that, she was an associate high school principal and staff development specialist at Urbandale High School in Iowa.

During her Urbandale experience, she worked closely with staff members, Grant Wiggins, and Bruce Joyce over a two-year period to implement performance assessment into the high school. While she was at the intermediate agency and Ankeny, she received extensive training in curriculum mapping, Understanding by Design, and use of multiple forms of assessments from Heidi Hayes Jacobs, Bena Kallick, and Grant Wiggins. She can be contacted by e-mail at ann@ankeny.k12.ia.us.

Jennie L. Johnson taught English and language arts for more than 20 years in Minnesota and Iowa. She is now a curriculum and assessment specialist with the Ankeny Community School District in Ankeny, Iowa. As part of her current position, Jennie assists with implementing the curriculum mapping process and oversees the training for and implementing of the database software that will contain the curriculum maps, lesson plans, and performance tasks with scoring tools in the district.

As part of curriculum mapping, she has assisted the secondary school in integrating reading and writing skills into the maps and has helped design training in reading and writing strategies for all secondary staff members. In addition, she has worked with administrators and staff members in analyzing data from the curriculum mapping process and district assessments to determine the need for professional development in instructional strategies within the district.

She can be contacted by e-mail at jennie@ankeny.k12.ia.us.

Bena Kallick is a private consultant who provides services to school districts, state departments of education, professional organizations, and public agencies throughout the United States and abroad. She received her doctorate in educational evaluation at Union Graduate School. Her written work includes *Changing Schools into Communities for Thinking* (1999, Technology Pathways);

Assessment in the Learning Organization (1995, ASCD), coedited with Arthur Costa; *Habits of Mind* (2000, ASCD), a four-book series coauthored with Arthur Costa; and *Information Technology for Schools: Creating Practical Knowledge to Improve Student Performance* (2001, Jossey-Bass), coauthored with James M. Wilson III. Her most recent book, coauthored with Arthur Costa, is *Assessment Strategies for Self-Directed Learning* (2003, Corwin Press Publishers). She can be contacted at Bena@techpaths.com.

Joseph Lachowicz has been principal for 10 years of the Allegheny Intermediate Unit (AIU). During the past 4 years, he has been principal for the Alternative Education Program (AEP) of the AIU. His responsibilities include supervising the educational program of a juvenile detention center and of the Allegheny County Jail, plus supervising three county shelter programs that work with neglected and delinquent youths. He implemented curriculum mapping 4 years ago at all of his schools. He teaches both induction classes on curriculum mapping for new teachers and credit courses on curriculum mapping and research-based instructional strategies approved through the Department of Education in Pennsylvania. He can be contacted at jlachowicz@aep .lcn.net.

Michael Lucas, formerly an elementary school principal, now serves as principal of Dutch Fork Middle School in Irmo, South Carolina. He is enrolled in the Ed.D. program at Seton Hall University and can be contacted at mlucas@lex5.k12.sc.us.

Stephen D. O'Neil is the upper school principal at Minnehaha Academy, a private school in Minneapolis, Minnesota. In his previous position as director of curriculum (PreK–12), he led Minnehaha Academy through the adoption and implementation of curriculum mapping. He presents workshops around the country, training faculty and administrators in how to achieve school excellence through curriculum mapping.

Claire Thompson is principal of Lake Murray Elementary School in South Carolina's District Five. She can be contacted at cthompso@lex5.k12.sc.us.

Valerie Truesdale led South Carolina's District Five in the curriculum mapping initiative as the chief instructional services officer. She was assisted in the initiative by a pair of dynamic principals: Mike Lucas and Claire Thompson. Dr. Truesdale currently serves as superintendent of Oconee County Schools in South Carolina and on the ASCD Board of Directors. She can be contacted at vtruesdale@oconee.k12.sc.us.

James M. Wilson III specializes in knowledge management and is the founder and director of Data and Decision Analysis, a management-consulting firm that develops decision support systems. He has conducted research with the National Center of Education Statistics, the U.S. Department of Education's Regional Laboratories, the Southern Regional Education Board, and numerous other public and private education research organizations. Over the past 20 years, he has worked directly with 17 state educational agencies, as well as numerous school districts, to improve their data-collection practices, management of policy information, and knowledge creation. Dr. Wilson can be reached by e-mail at jameswilson@data decision.com.

Related ASCD Resources

At the time of publication, the following ASCD resources were available; for the most up-to-date information about ASCD resources, go to www.ascd.org. ASCD stock numbers are noted in parentheses.

Audio

Control Versus Autonomy: Dilemma in a Time of Change and Accountability by Marian Leibowitz (Audiotape #204092)

Curriculum Mapping: A Tool for Instructional Decision Making by Chris Stewart (Audiotape #203080)

Succeeding with Standards: Linking Curriculum, Assessment, and Action Planning by Judy F. Carr and Douglas E. Harris (Audiotape #202237)

Print Products

Curriculum Technology Quarterly, Spring 2003: Connecting Curriculum Mapping and Technology (#103310)

Educational Leadership, December 2003/January 2004: New Needs, New Curriculum (#104026)

Mapping the Big Picture: Integrating Curriculum and Assessment K–12 by Heidi Hayes Jacobs (#197135)

Succeeding with Standards: Linking Curriculum, Assessment, and Action Planning by Judy F. Carr and Douglas E. Harris (#101005)

For more information, visit us on the World Wide Web (http://www.ascd.org), send an e-mail message to member@ascd.org, call the ASCD Service Center (1-800-933-ASCD or 703-578-9600, then press 2), send a fax to 703-575-5400, or write to Information Services, ASCD, 1703 N. Beauregard St., Alexandria, VA 22311-1714 USA.